MW01139672

THE
VALUE
ENTERPRISE

The Value Enterprise is co-published by McGraw-Hill Ryerson, a subsidiary of the McGraw-Hill Companies, and Report on Business Magazine, Canada's leading business magazine. Report on Business Magazine and McGraw-Hill Ryerson are committed to publishing leading edge business trends and management books.

THE
VALUE
ENTERPRISE

Strategies for Building a Value-Based Organization

JOHN DONOVAN
RICHARD TULLY   BRENT WORTMAN

 **McGraw-Hill Ryerson**

TORONTO   NEW YORK   BURR RIDGE   BANGKOK   BOGOTA
CARACAS   LISBON   LONDON   MADRID   MEXICO CITY
MILAN   NEW DELHI   SEOUL   SINGAPORE   SYDNEY   TAIPEI

McGraw-Hill
Ryerson Limited

A Subsidiary of The **McGraw·Hill** *Companies*

300 Water Street, Whitby, Ontario L1N 9B6
http://www.mcgrawhill.ca

THE VALUE ENTERPRISE

ISBN: 0-07-552816-9

2 3 4 5 6 7 8 9 0 TRI 9 0 1 9 8 7 6 5 4 3 2 1 0 9 8

Printed and bound in Canada

Care has been taken to trace ownership of copyright material contained in this text; however, the publisher will welcome any information that enables them to rectify any reference or credit for subsequent editions.

Canadian Cataloguing in Publication Data

Tully, Richard, 1958-
   The value enterprise: strategies for building a value-based organization
(Report on business)
Includes index.
ISBN 0-07-552816-9
1. Managerial economics 2. Value. I. Donovan, John, 1960- . II. Title.
III. Series: Report on Business (Whitby, Ont.).
HD30.22.T85 1997   658   C96-931306-3

Publisher: **Joan Homewood**
Editor: **Erin Moore**
Production Coordinator: **Jennifer Burnell**
Editorial Services: **Ron Edwards**
Cover Design: **Art Plus**
Interior Design/Composition: **Pages Design**
Printer: **Tri-Graphic Printing Ltd.**

Credits

The authors and publisher of this volume wish to acknowledge the following sources of material: Tables from Edward A. Robinson, *FORTUNE*, copyright © 1997 Time Inc., New York. All rights reserved. Reprinted with permission. Tables from Reports #1114-95-RR p. 12 and 1113-95-RR p.15,16,19, The Conference Board, New York, 1995. Reprinted with permission.

CONTENTS

LIST OF FIGURES

FOREWORD
by
Barry Hedley

This book goes to the heart of how managers can most effectively implement the principles of "Value-Based Management" in their corporations. Value-Based Management is a rather new development in management thinking. Popularized by terms such as "Economic Value Added" and "Cash Flow Return on Investment," it focuses all people in a company on the common goal of creating value for its constituents. It is no exaggeration to say that, when well applied, this simple concept can literally transform a company's strategy and operations, throughout the entire organization. It can provide a new and invigorating rallying cry for managers jaded and dispirited from years of downsizing. It can generate positive teamwork from groups of disparate managers previously driven by interdepartmental rivalries and diverging objectives. It does this by "depoliticizing" the management process and uniting all management efforts towards the pursuit of a common, objective, external goal: the maximization of value over the long term.

However, as with many excellent ideas, gaining the promised benefits in practice is far from straightforward. That is where this book helps. Drawing from a wealth of research and—more importantly—practical experience, the authors show, with plentiful examples, how companies can achieve a transition to a dynamic, value-driven enterprise. The lessons and approaches they advocate merit serious consideration, both by newcomers to value-based management, and also by those who already have more than a passing familiarity with the concept.

A few words of background may be helpful. Having spent much of my own working life helping managers wrestle with issues of corporate and business unit strategy, I personally find value-based management particularly exciting because it very neatly closes a gap in strategy thinking. As a serious, analytical, management discipline, "strategy" has now been practised for around 30 years. It rests on the concept that business success requires, not just understanding markets and delighting customers with products and services that they value, but ***doing this better, and/or at lower cost, than competitors.*** Unless this is achieved, the business can not be expected to generate good economic results. However, until value-based management arrived, we really had no sound way of measuring whether this result had actually been achieved. Most managers measured financial results using generally accepted accounting principles, looking at profits or, perhaps, return on capital employed. Generally, reported profits were regarded as good, losses as bad. Of course, this is not a bad starting point. However, the principles of VBM suggest that this is too limited a concept. *"Good" economic performance is only achieved when the rate of profit earned on invested capital exceeds the company's cost of capital.*

This is essentially an "outperforming competitors" *financial concept*, since the "cost of capital" essentially represents the return the investor could achieve if investing in alternative companies in the capital markets (after due allowance for differences in risk).

Thus there is an elegant symmetry between successful competitive business strategy—outperforming competitors in the commercial market place for products and services—and the results in terms of successful financial performance—outperforming the alternative investments available to the investor in the capital market place. In a value-driven enterprise, everyone integrates these "two sides of the same coin," intimately and virtually instinctively, everywhere from the boardroom to the shop floor.

This book does not fall into the common trap of most others written on the topic of managing for value. It does not ensnare the reader in the complexities of alternative value "metrics," the technical details of cost of capital determination, and other matters more properly the province of specialist financial managers. Nor does it focus on the essentially passive and uncreative activity of mere value *measurement*. Instead, it concentrates on showing how line managers, whether general managers or functional managers, can come to grips with identifying the business and operational drivers which they can control and how to operate them in ways which will lead to value *creation*.

Importantly, the book shows that value creation need not be limited simply to shareholder value, but can and should also be linked explicitly to the creation of value for customers, and for the company's employees. This perspective is extremely valuable in an environment where some observers may believe—erroneously—that creation of value for the investors in an enterprise is some sort of "zero-sum game," whereby shareholder value maximization is somehow only to be achieved by reducing product quality or customer service, or by cutting the remuneration of employees.

Instead, the authors show how management processes can be developed to ensure the *simultaneous* maximization of investor, customer and employee value—reflecting the fact that an economically and competitively successful business will typically reinforce its success by the provision of *better* products and customer service, and will further consolidate this by rewarding its employees *better* than its competitors, thereby attracting *better* people to its ranks, enabling it in turn to generate yet *better* commercial and financial performance.

At the heart of this practical value creation process is the approach the authors describe as "value modeling." This involves managers exploring in depth the interaction between the business drivers they control and the likely impact variations in those drivers will have on value. These value models can vary in complexity from simple logic frameworks designed to structure and guide qualitative thought, to fully interlinked mathematical models with attractive user-friendly input screens and graphical output. At whatever level they are constructed, however, they share the objective of helping managers develop a deep understanding of how the decisions they take and the external factors impacting their business, will affect value. This results not only in more creative option assessment and planning for business; it also leads to more effective day-to-day management of business operations, which are continually redirected toward long-term value maximization.

This book therefore fills an important gap, linking the theory of Value-Based Management to its effective practice. Following the approaches described will help managers to produce a profound transformation in the way they plan and operate their businesses, leading to value creation for all the interested constituencies: investors, customers and employees. *The Value Enterprise* provides a benchmark towards which all management planning, operations, performance measurement, reward and control processes should aspire.

Barry Hedley
Group Chairman, Braxton Associates
The Strategy Consulting Practice
Deloitte & Touche Consulting Group
London, England
June 1997

ACKNOWLEDGEMENTS

The creation of this book has itself been a Value Journey. Created over a long period while we were consulting in the field and implementing our ideas during the day, the book got written on nights and weekends. As you would expect, we received lots of help and insightful comments throughout the process that both clarified the thinking and helped to finish the work involved.

We would first like to thank our wives and families: Susan, Jaclyn, Judy, Rory, Shaina, Karen, Oliver, Roxanne and Jason. Without their support we could never have got to this point. Next, there are a large number of colleagues who made significant contributions. At the risk of missing someone, the contributors were:

Rick Blaiklock, Nancy Vanden Bosch, Todd Crick, Lloyd Switzer, Scott Blackwell, Jeanine Madder, Kurt Wolf, Firdhaus Pohowahla, Krishna Tyagarajan, Geoff George, Annette Brennan, Susan Schwartz, Mike McConnell, Rob Reynolds, Phil Strause, Stephen Sprinkle, Johanna Millers, Susie Goan, Tina Mollo, Jared Mitchell, Ron Edwards and, of course, the Modelheads.

We would also like to thank Joan Homewood and the people at McGraw-Hill Ryerson for their patience and support.

Chapter 1

VALUE-BASED MANAGEMENT

A Framework for Enterprise Value

The forces of change are demanding that organizations transform themselves if they are to survive. Technology and globalization are creating such intense competition that only the strong will carry on for the long term. Most organizations have begun to recognize the need for change and have started the journey. Consultants and academics have provided tools like TQM, reengineering and change management but still many struggle to change.

Over the past several years we have observed that one of the key issues with most organizations is a lack of clarity in what they are trying to become and how they manage their way to their goal. Clearly the old command and control management process doesn't work, but what is to replace it? Many organizations are now measuring shareholder value creation as a goal, but few have integrated value into their management process. Others have embraced customer focus as their key driver, while still others are focusing on competencies as a means of creating competitive advantage.

Which of these new approaches is likely to be successful in the future? In our view the answer is all of them and none of them. To be truly successful in the new world, organizations must be able to create value for all of their key constituencies by managing to create win-wins rather than trading one off against the other. This view must also be completely baked into all aspects of the management process from planning and analysis, to measurement and decision making, if it is to take hold and transform how the company is managed.

Organizations are now experiencing this process of managing for enterprise value and are becoming value enterprises. The journey is not easy but it is a necessary one if organizations are to survive long term. In this book we will show you examples of companies who are making this transition and the success it is providing them. We will also illustrate the things you can do to begin this journey yourself.

Perhaps the best place to start is with a company that is truly on the path to becoming a value enterprise.

By the early 1990s Boeing Corp. had enjoyed three-quarters of a century of success. Its name was known around the world, virtually synonymous with commercial aviation. Indeed, one would be hard-pressed to find an air traveler anywhere on the globe who hadn't been aboard a Boeing aircraft—many times. Founded in Seattle in 1916 by William Edward Boeing, an early aviation buff, the company grew to dominate the international aircraft manufacturing market. But by 1994, it began to encounter difficulty.

It was one of those defining moments that people point to later as the turning point, an indication that "Big Things" were about to happen. Northwest Airlines had decided to refurbish their ancient fleet of 40 DC-9s. The kicker was that they would not be buying Boeing's 737s. The $2-billion deal, which, at times, seemed almost a sure thing, was out the window. And to make matters worse, the Northwest refit—at a cost of only $200-million— meant that their fleet would have an extended life of another 15 years.

1994 was not a happy year for the Seattle airplane giant. Revenues were only $22 billion, down from $31 just two years earlier, and earnings were off by nearly half to $856 million. Boeing was forced to cut 9,300 jobs, nearly 14 percent of its workforce. The previous year, Moody's had downgraded Boeing's senior debt rating (from double-A-3 to single-A-1) for the first time in the company's history. How had things come to this point for the world-renowned aerospace leader?

Boeing often felt itself at the mercy of the wildly unpredictable commercial airline industry. With deregulation in the 1970s, that industry had become even more unpredictable, as fierce competition drove down prices and profit margins and drove many carriers into the ground. The wake-up call, from Northwest Airlines, came just in time. As CEO Frank Shrontz, said, "We were using the challenge of competing with the used airplane as a rallying call."[1]

Shrontz and President Philip Condit, set about building value for their company, taking steps that would rebuild Boeing's warranted value. They began, in effect, to do the things required to effectively balance the need to generate an appropriate return to shareholders with the needs of their other key constituents—customers and employees.

To turn around Boeing, Condit and Shrontz, in effect, installed a value-based approach to management. Although they did not consciously set out to create a value enterprise, they took many of the right actions. Their strategic goal was to create positive shareholder value over the long term. To do that they had to shake things up. The company had become a little too complacent.

Boeing had seen trouble on the horizon when it launched the 777 project in 1990. Before committing the billions needed to develop a brand new family of passenger aircraft—what Condit has called "the largest privately funded endeavor in the world"[2]—Boeing did its homework. Step one was to talk to their customers: what did they want and need in a new airplane? What would they be needing in a decade, in a quarter century? They practiced what Phil Condit calls "aggressive listening." Their first move was to bring together airlines from around the globe, long before any designs were begun, and convince them to share their needs with Boeing.

With the 777, Boeing's goal was to create "the most advanced jetliner on the market," but, at the same time, to completely revamp its design and manufacturing process. At the time, Boeing was still doing things in the "proven" ways. But these proven ways were outmoded, often dating back to World War II. Much of Boeing's problem stemmed from its own success. During World War II, when the company grew by leaps and bounds, Boeing produced tens of thousands of B-17s and B-29s, and continued on in the fifties and sixties, mass-producing a few models of superb aircraft for wealthy airlines which lined up for its products. By the eighties and nineties, customers had become more demanding. Airlines were now calling for specialized, customized products, not suited to the production line mentality stemming from World War II. "We used to build planes in the classic serial fashion," says Michael Boyce,

Boeing's director of business development. "We didn't find most of the mistakes until we built the product. Some 30 percent of the cost was wasted effort."[3]

With the 777 project, headed by Condit from the beginning, the traditional development practices of dozens of design teams working on various parts of the aircraft, virtually in isolation, came to an end. When analyzed, Boeing discovered that the old ways were not only slow and inefficient, they led to tremendous amounts of duplicated efforts and unnecessary redesigns when the specs from one isolated engineering team conflicted with that of another.

The old isolated design teams were replaced by a unified "design-build" team using the latest computer-assisted design and inventory control. The result was that the team working on say, wing design, got immediate feedback from the fuel, electrical and hydraulics teams as they proceeded. All could make adjustments and discuss changes during the process, rather than having to redesign things later when one team's specs didn't jibe with another's. The new system allowed for a maximum of flexibility in design process, and customization was no longer the major headache it once was.

And the changes at Boeing went beyond the modernization and integration of the design and manufacturing process. When Frank Shrontz took over as CEO in 1986, it was in the midst of one of the largest booms in airplane manufacturing history. A lawyer with an MBA from Harvard, Shrontz was able to see the need for change. But he admits that the problem wasn't an easy one, "Trying to change this company without a crisis wasn't easy. We had 75 years of history, and we were very successful. There was a strong feeling of 'Why change?'"[4]

But Shrontz changed and forced changes on the corporation. He forced everyone to meet, talk and listen—across departmental lines. The engineers and techies had to try to understand the concerns of the sales, marketing, finance, customer support and operations departments, and vice versa. As Shrontz's copilot, and his replacement as CEO, Phil Condit commented, "You can put someone from the finance department next to a structural engineer, and they'll have no idea what the other guy is talking about. The easy solution is to put up higher barriers and not share information. The better idea is to bring varied skills together and begin to understand each other. When it works well, you have a lot more power."[5]

The large, complex integration of systems in the production process is mirrored throughout the corporate culture. So, just as they broke down the barriers between the various design and production teams in the new 777 production process, barriers fell throughout Boeing. Departments began, reluctantly at first, to share information and learn one another's needs. The changes begun by Shrontz have been expanded and built upon by Condit, a firm believer in teamwork. As Condit commented, "I found people who wanted to contribute but didn't think anyone was listening."[6] He listened.

Despite a retooling of the production and planning process, along with the corporate culture, strains were inevitable. In the fall of 1995, Boeing's workforce staged a strike for increased wages and job security. Ever the communicator, Condit became concerned that the ten-week strike would damage Boeing's "team culture." As Bob Watt, chairman of the Seattle Chamber of Commerce, explained, "Boeing's labor negotiators probably didn't like it, but he just went out and talked to the picketers." Adds Watt, "I think that was the beginning of the end of the strike."[7]

Condit had succeeded in creating a value enterprise by getting his customers fully involved in the design and manufacturing process of the revolutionary new Boeing 777. They were consulted before the process was even begun and through every stage. Suppliers were likewise drawn into the system, and the "team culture" promoted by Boeing led to the involvement of the workforce, not only in traditional feedback, but in every stage of the planning and manufacturing process. Employees share in the success of the company through the "ShareValue Trust," established in 1996, through which employees participate in Boeing's share price appreciation.

All three constituencies win through Condit's commitment to "customer satisfaction, shareholder value and teamwork."

Over the past three decades, organizations have pursued a number of approaches advocated by business theorists. Some of these have included: Total Quality Management, Customer Satisfaction, Business Process Reengineering, and Activity-Based Costing. But none of these approaches fully addresses the complete needs of a business. They are useful to a point or in parts of a business, but they fail to establish holistic solutions to problems. The thoughtful manager will ask some fundamental questions when looking for a solution.

The first question is: "Why does my organization even exist?" It must have a business concept that incorporates products and services that have a unique value proposition for its intended market. The concept must fill a customer need in price-to-quality terms that is unique relative to its competition. Secondly, it must have employees who believe in the organization and who are willing to make the company successful while receiving a valuable experience both financially and personally over the long term. Thirdly, it must have investors who believe in the business concept and the people and who are therefore willing to invest their money in the future success of the organization. Without all of these three pieces the organization probably will not stay in existence for long.

While all organizations want to create value for all their key constituents—customers, employees and shareholders—very few can sustain this over the long term. Success is about creating win-wins and that's very difficult. In fact, few organizations do it. Value-based management is a framework which can make it easier. Many companies do not even realize there is a problem until it's too late, forced into major restructuring or ending up in bankruptcy. Like poor wiring behind the walls, the problem often goes unnoticed until disaster strikes.

If a company is committed to creating value for all stakeholders, how could it possibly lose its way? The fundamental reason is that companies lack a complete and comprehensive framework for managing themselves relative to their reasons for being—creating value for all stakeholders. Any successful approach to management must address the fundamental reasons for the existence of an organization. Value-based management is the comprehensive framework. This book describes a framework and approach that explicitly addresses managing the fundamental reasons for being. Real-life examples and fictitious illustrations of management problems experienced in our consulting assignment will show how companies are taking the journey to becoming a value enterprise and how others can take this journey too.

How do companies take the journey to becoming a value enterprise? There is a proven approach to making this goal a reality for any organization: the Value Journey™. The Value Journey addresses the key elements: culture, management infrastructure and competency. The Value Journey is a long, complex and difficult undertaking. Creating a value enterprise means taking the journey across all functional boundaries in an organization and involving all constituencies. But just as managing a business is not a one-dimensional undertaking, neither is a comprehensive approach to value creation. This means that progress is often revealed unevenly and in fits and starts. What makes the complexity manageable is the powerful, accommodating, and comprehensive framework of this approach that is not offered by any other value methodologies. This comprehensive value framework works with four segments in an organization:

- senior management

- middle management

- process and operations management

- rank and file

The first segment is senior management. The value-based framework benefits the highest levels of a company with its broad focus and specific emphasis on implementation. Often, senior managers are exposed only to the high-level, conceptual view of any initiative, and then again to the compensation level.

Figure 1.1   The Value Journey™

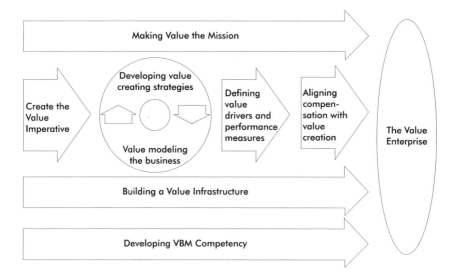

Senior management is usually part of the front and back end of any given plan, but has no real exposure to the middle implementation phase. This results in misperceptions and mistakes. Because the value-based framework is comprehensive and concentrates on implementation, senior management immediately benefits from a broad view of the entire operation.

The next segment is middle management. The value approach in this book offers middle managers hands-on insights into the "how-to" of creating value. Numerous general concepts exist for why value should be created, and many organizations have adopted them. But on a regular basis middle managers are enormously frustrated by the lack of comprehensive information about execution of the concepts. Most middle managers are told by senior executives to achieve a value focus, but remarkably, they are given very little actual instruction on how to go about it, resulting in gaps in communication and understanding. Senior management also commonly fails to display the patience needed to see the whole process through. So middle managers end up with the responsibility for creating value, often with their compensation tied to it in some way, but without crucial learning and support. A comprehensive value framework provides middle managers with a tangible set of tools for comprehension and implementation of value concepts that are consistent with their spheres of influence.

The third segment is process and operations management. This includes the people in charge of accounts payable, accounts receivable and warehouse and inventory management. This segment has the most to gain from a comprehensive value framework. Traditionally, when a company adopts any new management trend or initiative, operations is the area of the company that is most noticeably whip sawed into putting it in place. It usually happens without the necessary support and articulation from middle management because they themselves have not been properly prepared. Process and operations managers often receive a high-level view of the current management flavor of the month with all of its promise, but without a complete understanding or recognition by upper management of the complexities involved in day to day implementation at the operations level. The problem is everywhere. Process managers continue to express a tremendous frustration with new trend (including value) programs that result in their having to change their management process without a comprehensive understanding of why or how.

The fourth and final segment is the rank and file—the front line workers at the warehouse, on the manufacturing line, and behind the retail counter. A comprehensive value framework touches them by recognizing that organizational competency and value creation are driven primarily by people. In other words, value is determined deep inside operations by how well people at the front line do their jobs. A company creates value in the boiler room and counts it in the penthouse. This emphasis on the contribution made by the rank and file in every organization sets this value approach apart from all others.

And yet many firms do not realize how far into the organization they must extend the understanding of value creation. Deloitte & Touche Consulting Group has introduced value-based compensation measures extensively to human resources (HR) departments. On the whole they have embraced the measures, but there is a common negative comment: "How can employees be motivated to create value if they don't understand how to contribute to its creation?" It is precisely in those situations that value-based compensation can have the most impact. The very notion that a company could be full of people who don't understand how they contribute to value creation should be unacceptable to any business. Yet this is indeed the case in a vast majority of companies, and in fact is the very reason why the whole concept of value-based management came about. Only when people understand their role in an organization and clearly perceive how they can contribute to value, is value creation going to take place on any significant scale.

Companies often ask us: "How well are we doing with respect to Value-Based Management?" In response to this we developed a simple diagnostic tool called The Value Aptitude Test to gauge their Value IQ. Figure 1.2 illustrates this simple test that allows you to assess where you are and your progress along the Value Journey.

Boeing is not alone in creating superb value. The case of the Canadian software firm Cognos is equally instructive. Incorporated in 1969, the Ottawa firm consulted to the Canadian government and customized software for it. But its ambition to branch out into international markets and to switch its product

Figure 1.2   Value Aptitude Test

1. Does my organization look for solutions that simultaneously improve value for customers, employees and shareholders, or are we constantly evaluating tradeoffs?

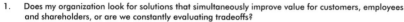

2. Does my organization approach customer and employee performance measurement as rigorously as it does financial measurement?

3. Are decisions made using fact-based analysis, or do we "mine data" to support our intuition?

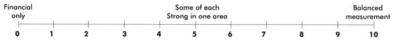

4. Do we have a quantitative understanding of how the business works as a system, not just as a collection of parts?

5. Do we have a deep understanding of the value drivers of our business, their thresholds and their interactions with all aspects of the business?

6. Is there an integrated performance measurement framework that links from an individual level to the corporate level and covers employee, investor and customer interactions?

7. Is compensation linked to value creation or tenure? Do individuals understand how they contribute to value and get paid for its creation?

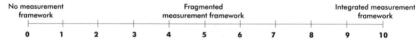

8. Does the planning process adapt to market dynamics or does the "budget" represent management's social contract with the organization?

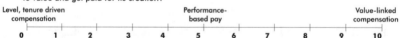

9. Does the data, process and competency infrastructure support a fast and flexible organization or do "one-off" reports and projects drive the organization?

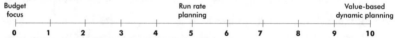

10. How does the organization rank against other companies, both inside and outside the industry, in value created for shareholders, customers and employees?

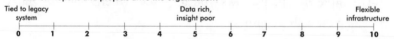

line to application-development software proved difficult. It had a solid product: its PowerHouse was well respected and enjoyed strong customer loyalty.

But Cognos began to experience several years of harsh losses, with new products failing to realize their potential. The company's executives discovered that their organization was not as keenly attuned as they had thought to the fast-evolving world of software. Ron Zambonini, then president and chief operating officer, told shareholders in the 1994 annual report, "We had a substantial infrastructure, and were heavily dependent on a large direct sales force. While this suited selling into our proprietary business, it wasn't efficient enough, and we felt it hindered our ability to pursue new opportunities and grow our position within the client-server and desktop markets."[8]

Migrating to business intelligence software from its former function allowed Cognos to become a market leader with its PowerPlay and Impromptu products. It maintains this lead by continuously focusing on creating value for its customers by enhancing its products and developing new ones to meet their needs. With the business-intelligence software business growing 73 percent between 1993 and 1997, Cognos came out on top, growing sales by 163 percent by fiscal 1995. A 1995 survey by Forrester Research identified Cognos as one of the five most strategic vendors of data access for *FORTUNE 1000* companies, putting it in the company of IBM, Microsoft, and Oracle. For shareholders who had held on through the lean years, value began to be realized. Its stock price headed up to the $40 range on NASDAQ after hovering between $10 and $20 for several years. 1996 was even more successful: net income topped $23 million on sales that grew by 25 percent. In 1996, its shares soared toward $80 and the company announced a three-for-one split in the stock. During the five years ended December 1996, the company produced average total shareholder returns of 53.3 percent.

How did it achieve this? Cognos went to extraordinary lengths to service its customers and ensure real value creation. It maintains a "Customer Visit" program that invites 70 customers to Cognos offices throughout the world to exchange ideas with software engineers and senior executives. It organizes conferences around the world that bring together customers, partners, and employees to share product expertise. It also created a "Customer Advisory Board" to provide a platform for exchanging information among key cus-

tomers. It enables Cognos to understand its customers' needs and to incorporate ideas into future generations of software. It even employs a voting system
for product improvement so customers can have a say in the priority of proposed changes in software. Cognos then tries to incorporate the changes voted
most important by its customers in the next version.

The company has also excelled with creating value for employees as
well. It removed management layers and mandated business units and field
managers to direct their own corners of the business, making the overall operation lean, effective and more stimulating for employees. It has broken down
the walls between different departments with cross-functional teams that
bring various expertise to bear on product challenges throughout the entire
life cycle of a product.

Cognos offers excellent salaries and benefits but in a highly competitive environment for people recognize the need to create a positive work
environment. People are encouraged to challenge conventional wisdom
and to follow creative ideas without fear of criticism. Flexible work
arrangements and multiple career tracks provide the opportunity for all
people to contribute and succeed. Cognos also encourages fitness and ath-
leticism through an on-site gym.

It's clear that Cognos has created tremendous value for its shareholders
over the past five years and thanks to its concentration on solid value creation it
has benefited its employees and customers as well. In 1996, Zambonini told
the *Ottawa Citizen* that his goal is to reach $1 billion in annual sales within
five years.[9] It is an entirely credible goal, given the company's track record.

The kind of success that Cognos and Boeing have enjoyed can be
duplicated. The blueprint for creating a Value Enterprise lies in the pages
ahead. Here is an overview of how to begin a successful Value Journey.

Chapter Two looks at the issue of Enterprise Value. Without this understanding any management approach will be too simplistic and shortsighted.
This chapter illustrates the need to create value for all stakeholders for the
long term. It demonstrates that creating value is not about trade-offs
between stakeholders but rather finding strategies that create value for all.

In Chapter Three, the key first step in the Value Journey, Making Value
Your Mission is addressed. Clearly, any transformation of the nature intended

by the Value Journey must be fully ingrained into the fabric of the organization. This chapter provides through example, how this can occur and why it is so critical. A commitment toward creating value must be built. It must be the mission, so central to any organization that it stands out from your competitors because the marketplace sees it as providing exemplary value and quality.

The Enterprise Value Scorecard (Chapter Four) examines the importance of measurement for assessing the performance of an organization. The value scorecard is critical because it becomes the language by which value is discussed and managed. How does a company analyze value? Is it still looking at last year's figures to predict where it will be creating value next year? That is like backing into the future. Businesses that continue to rely on the convenience and familiarity of traditional accounting numbers are doing themselves a disservice. Traditional accounting measures are priceless for reporting past progress. But a forward-looking approach is necessary to see where the value is coming from, or where it is being frustrated, or overlooked. To complicate matters, not just the financial outcomes must be considered but also the value created for other stakeholders like customers and employees. This clearly makes the value scorecard a key issue.

Chapter Five, Value Modeling brings us to the heart of putting value-based management to work. Value modeling is one of the preeminent tools for understanding how customers, employees, and shareholders relate with each other. Chapter Five explores modeling in detail, explaining the main components of a value model, including assets, activities, processes, and modules for customer and employee value. The value model connects these components and their basic elements through a wide variety of mathematical relationships. The purpose of the model is not to predict the future, but rather to understand how the myriad elements of the business relate to one another and work to create value. Because value models are not predictive, they typically employ various likely scenarios of the future to understand how the business and its existing strategies would fare under each scenario. Sensitivity analysis, applied to each of the model's elements, can reveal the components that have the greatest impact on value. Also known as value drivers, these components ought to be the focus of a company that is managing for value and, therefore, should be established as the performance measures by which the company operates. Benchmarking can be employed to set targets for these value-based performance measures. The value model can be used to assess the value to be realized from achieving the performance targets. The model can also be used to assess the value impacts of strategies that are developed for the business.

Where is value being created? What are the strategies that will create value for all stakeholders rather than forcing trade-offs? The quick answer is often not the best answer. And that is an important realization, since far too many managers actually destroy value because they have no way of knowing just what effect their decisions and policies have on all stakeholders. "Siloing" is the tendency of large corporations to operate their business units in isolation from each other. For example, what happens to the customer service activities of a long-distance telephone company when marketing decides to offer sign up incentives that prove wildly popular with consumers? Will customer service be swamped, and will that result in frustrated consumers becoming alienated when they cannot get through to that department with their problems? What are the impacts of the incentives on the telecommunications switching network? Can it handle the load or will customers get persistent busy signals? How would the effect of strategies like this be modeled?

Chapter Six addresses Value Drivers and Performance Measures — the currency that ensures that the right issues get addressed as part of ongoing management. Knowing how to model your company effectively will lead you to uncover what is driving value creation in terms of risks and opportunities and how it can be measured. Pinpointing value drivers can lead to using strategies that result in the largest improvement in cash flows, allowing a focus of energy and resources. By testing scenarios about its operating environment a company can identify the factors that drive value in its business and measure their impact on cash flow. In identifying and measuring its business, a company naturally focuses on what drives value.

Value-Based Compensation (Chapter Seven) tells companies how to create incentives for managers and employees to do the right things. Compensation can be aligned with value creation by tying the incentive component of compensation to the value-based performance measures.

In Chapter Eight, one of the key issues of making value real, Value-Based Planning is discussed. This chapter shows how value can be linked into the planning process, which is typically one of the keys to how businesses are managed.

Chapter Nine addresses the topic of the Value Infrastructure, which includes processes, tools and information needed to enable managers and employees to understand customer, employee and shareholder value and their interrelationships. Not only does value-based management enable a company to be run holistically but it identifies the tools with which to measure progress. In the oil business, what impact would a sudden world political crisis have on a business and how would it react? How soon could it react? Before its competitors? A value-based corporate infrastructure will help cope with such events.

The final chapter (Ten) discusses the Successful Value Enterprise and the Appendix compares the Value Enterprise with other popular management trends.

With the speed of business change today and a ferocity of competition that has become commonplace, any company faces serious peril unless it comes to grips with value creation and preservation. With a value-based management framework, as described in this book, the organization can have the tools to identify problems, to see how its different parts work to create or destroy value and how exactly it can remedy it problems.

ENTERPRISE VALUE

Creating Value for All Stakeholders

The Schlitz Brewing Company of Milwaukee, Wisconsin was a brewery that had a profitable product before it began looking for ways to reduce costs. In 1974, it began greatly shortening the brewing process. "Accelerated batch fermentation," developed over ten years, decreased beer fermentation from 12 to four days, significantly reducing costs and improving product uniformity. Then Schlitz had the idea to replace traditional barley malt with cheaper corn syrup. Although the taste of the beer was not seriously affected, word leaked out that Schlitz was moving its product out the door prematurely, selling what's known as "green beer." The perception was significant enough to alienate all but their most loyal customers.

At first, Schlitz's share price went up, thanks to its achievement of real savings. But once disgruntled beer drinkers started switching to other brands, the share price dropped. Schlitz had gambled that it could improve short-term operating cash flow by focusing only on cost-cutting, but management failed to analyze the effect on customer value. As illustrated in Figure 2.1, the company has yet to fully recover from the strategy.

Most companies define value in terms of particular dimensions: value for shareholders, customer intimacy or being operationally efficient. By definition this approach implies trade-offs between stakeholders that cause organizations to fall short of optimal value. Instead of trading off stakeholders, the most successful companies create enterprise value by creating value for all their stakeholders, customers, shareholders, employees, suppliers, the community and other entities. Successful companies find

Figure 2.1   Schlitz Beer Story

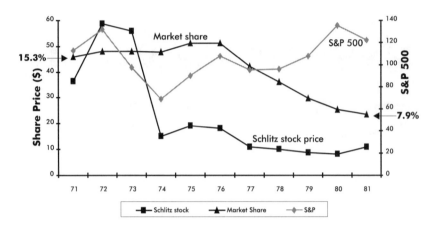

strategies that create win-win situations rather than trading off value among stakeholders.

Every company has three primary constituencies: customers, employees and shareholders. Because all three are subject to competition, every company must create enough value for each one in order to prosper. Unless all stakeholders receive sufficient value they will go elsewhere: customers will go to competitors, employees will go to work for them and investors will sell their stock. One stakeholder cannot be favored over the others without compromise. It's like a championship racing team, the car, driver and pit crew must all operate at peak performance to be successful.

The fact that value must be created for all stakeholders seems almost ridiculously obvious. But when you take a close look at what creating value for each of these stakeholders is all about, the challenge and enormous relevance in keeping them aligned is startling. As illustrated in Figure 2.2, the key is to understand fully what each stakeholder cares about and to deliver it in a way that creates win-win situations. In the long run, sustainable value will not be created for the enterprise unless all three stakeholder groups are an equal part of the value equation.

Managing for enterprise value is a big departure for many managers and, indeed, business theorists. They believe that catering to one or two constituencies will automatically guarantee that the others will be taken care of.

**Figure 2.2   Employees, Customers and Shareholders
Create Enterprise Value**

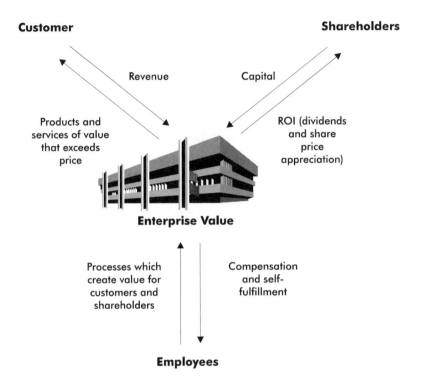

This is a grave mistake. Focusing on a single stakeholder is simplistic and shortsighted. You simply cannot sustain the creation of value if the needs of shareholders, customers and employees are not aligned. The importance of this becomes clear when it is recognized that a company's value and, by extension, its share price, are reflections of the company's ability to generate value over a long period of time. The best you can score in stakeholder trade-offs is to run standing still. Unforeseen cross-impacts between stakeholders mean that gains in one dimension, such as reduced costs, are almost always lost through reductions in others, as Schlitz's unintended loss of market share demonstrates.

A company must create value for all its stakeholders; it is the only proposition it can maintain successfully. Consider the link between profitability and customer value. In *The PIMS Principles, Linking Strategy to Performance*, Robert D. Buzzell and Bradley T. Gale define the profit impact of market strategy, or PIMS. Their book, based on the most extensive study relating strategy to profits and shareholder value, asserts that specific planning can help managers predict how strategic choices and market conditions would affect business performance: "In the long run, the most important single factor affecting a business unit's performance is the quality of its products and services, relative to those of competitors." [1]

Superior value is a mix of perceived quality and price, always relative to the competition. Figure 2.3 shows that businesses with superior products or services clearly out-perform those with inferior quality.

There are numerous other benefits that accrue to a business with perceived superior quality:

- Stronger customer loyalty

- More repeat purchases

- Less vulnerability to price wars

- Ability to command higher relative price without affecting market share

Figure 2.3   Quality Pays Off: The PIMS Findings on Relative Quality, Market Position and Cash Flow Generation

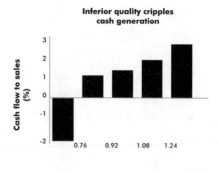

Source: PIMS database

- Lower marketing costs
- Market share improvements

Other stakeholders also play an important role in creating enterprise value. Key suppliers must also get value if the enterprise is to be successful in the long term. Squeezing their profit margins to reduce costs in the short term may reduce the viability of a supplier, creating negative impacts on the enterprise. On the other hand, joining forces can enable your business and your suppliers to create value. Abusing the environment to reduce costs in the short term will not be sustainable either. The community will eventually force the enterprise to fix the problem creating even greater costs. While these stakeholders are important, we will deal primarily with customers, employees and shareholders throughout this book. However, the concepts and principles we advocate for managing the value enterprise apply equally to other key stakeholders as well.

Clearly, shareholders, customers and employees are interrelated and strategies which do not address all three can be hazardous to an organization's health. One industry that has learned this lesson the hard way is retail. The 1970s and 1980s were horrendous years for retailers – roughshod competition, vast losses, bankruptcies, and other factors plagued the business sector. Famous and well-established retailers either vanished or shrank significantly during the onslaught: Kmart, the epoch-making F.W. Woolworth chain, and the venerable Canadian retailer Eaton's were gravely diminished. But throughout those turbulent 20 years one chain grew to preeminence, it is both admired by investors and feared by its competitors, a widely studied paradigm of successful retailing: Wal-Mart. Despite a few rough spots, they continue to perform for all constituencies at enviable levels.

Of the top ten discounters operating in 1962, the year that Wal-Mart opened its doors for business, not one remained in 1993. During those tough years Wal-Mart's store base grew to 2,440 outlets, and annual sales rose to $67.3 billion. The effect on its stock was a massive 19,807 percent increase. The company, based in Bentonville, Arkansas, has proven so successful in a contrary industry that its founder, Sam Walton, was the stuff of modern business legend. Entrepreneurs admired his success. Customers loved his prices relative to quality. Employees loved working for him. Competitors feared him to the point of irrationally seeking government help to block new stores from their towns.

Wal-Mart used no secret weapon to succeed in hard times, nor was it unique. Other companies in besieged industries have also done well: Southwest Airlines, poultry producer Tyson Foods, appliance and home-entertainment equipment retailer Circuit City and publisher Plenum Publishing all grew spectacularly between 1972 and 1992 as illustrated in Figure 2.4. Jeffrey Pffefer, in his book *Competitive Advantage Through People,*[2] noted that these companies were successful during those 20 years despite the fact that their industries had massive competition, horrendous losses, widespread bankruptcy, virtually no barriers to entry, little unique or proprietary technology, and many substitute products or services.

What they all did was balance their prevailing constituencies. Pffefer wrote: "For their sustained advantage they rely not on technology, patents or strategic position, but on how they manage their work force. The work force, and how it is organized and managed is an increasingly important source of competitive advantage."[3]

Just how did these companies create value at this outstanding rate? The answer lies in how they create value for each of their key constituencies. Let's take a closer look at each of the relationships with customers, employees, and shareholders.

Figure 2.4   Top Stock Market Performers 1972-92

Company	Industry	% Return
Southwest Airlines	Airline	21,775%
Wal-Mart	Discount retailer	19,807%
Tyson Foods	Poultry producer	18,118%
Circuit City	Video and appliance retailer	16,410%
Plenum Publishing	Publishing	15,689%

Source: adapted from *Competitive Advantage Through People*, Pfeffer, 1995

Customers

One of the most obvious but elusive relationships is the one a company has with its customers. Creating value for customers is simply delivering the best quality for price, relative to the competition. Customers will offer loyalty, patronage and dollars. In return, they want products and services with prices and a range of quality that they believe provide good value. A company earns a profit and market share if it keeps customers satisfied and loyal. The challenge is to offer significant value, whether the product is a Lexus or a Hyundai.

Wal-Mart's success in offering superior customer value is particularly instructive. Through innovative delivery and stocking techniques and open relationships with select vendors, Wal-Mart has beat the competition at providing low prices, which has translated in value for its shoppers. Suppliers deliver much of Wal-Mart's inventory directly to its stores, eliminating intermediate distribution and its associated cost. The company also introduced a process known as "cross-docking," which led to huge savings. Instead of placing merchandise from supplier's trucks into Wal-Mart's distribution centers, Wal-Mart began transferring merchandise straight from the supplier's trucks to Wal-Mart vehicles that were bound for its stores thereby reducing the amount of inventory sitting in Wal-Mart distribution centres. By 1994, 10 percent of Wal-Mart's merchandise was cross-docked at four specially equipped distribution facilities. Analysts estimated Wal-Mart's cost of inbound logistics to be significantly lower than its direct competitors, a cost advantage which amounted to almost 1 per cent of revenue. This resulted in millions of dollars in savings, much of which was ultimately passed on to the customer through lower prices. In 1993 Wal-Mart's operating expenses, as a percentage of sales were more than 7 percent lower than Kmart's. Indeed, Wal-Mart's cost savings between 1990 and 1993 ($2.2 billion) were greater than the $1.4 billion in net income for Kmart during the same period.

Wal-Mart also shrewdly shaved distribution costs with "backhauling." Many of Wal-Mart's vendors operate warehouses or factories within the retailer's territories. When an empty Wal-Mart truck drives by one of its suppliers on the way to or from a delivery, rather than going back empty to the distribution centre for its next load, the trucks stop and pick up merchandise for delivery to the Wal-Mart warehouse. This accelerates delivery and saves millions in shipping costs that Wal-Mart would otherwise pay to its suppliers. Wal-Mart's fleet of more than 2,000 trucks backhauled on 60 per cent of their journeys. Again, the direct savings showed up in lower prices in the store.

Wal-Mart's relationship with its suppliers also created value for customers. Over time, Wal-Mart whittled its vendor relationships down to partnerships with key suppliers. An important element of that partnerships is sharing information electronically. Since 1990, Wal-Mart's "retail link" has given more than 2,000 suppliers computer access to valuable point-of-sale data, used to analyze sales trends and inventory of their products store by store. It is not unusual for a Wal-Mart vendor to create an on-the-spot promotion in answer to a competitor's pricing strategy. The process translates into up-to-the-minute, razor-sharp competitive pricing which of course benefits shoppers. It also reinforces Wal-Mart's image of having always the lowest price. Value was created for shoppers through innovative delivery techniques and vendor relationships and it was delivered in the form of ultracompetitive pricing.

Employees

Far too many companies still look upon employees as a cost, not an asset. The *Minneapolis Star Tribune*, in a business ethics column,[4] asked if workers should matter as much as stockholders. The columnist asserted that in a year of record increases in the Dow Jones, record profits for investors and a whopping average annual return of 33 percent for hundreds of corporations, workers were the only constituency not sharing the wealth. With productivity climbing faster than real worker compensation in 1995, virtually none of those annual returns were passing down to employees. The columnist concluded that maximizing shareholder return has simply come to mean "squeeze the employees and give the gains to speculators."

Are workers as important as investors? They are in companies that are consistently successful in creating value. Value-based management requires that employees be inextricably linked and balanced with shareholders and customers in creating enterprise value. They are the stewards of the shareholders' investment. They must matter for a company to be viable. Without a motivated and contributing workforce, it's virtually impossible for a company to do well over the long term. As stakeholders in the company, employees offer their time, personal sacrifice, commitment and creativity. In return, they expect fair compensation, a challenging place in which to work, and the opportunity to learn, develop and advance. They also expect reasonable job satisfaction. In turn, the company will enjoy loyal, productive, innovative employees who help develop a competitive advantage.

As Jeffery Pffefer noted in his study, competitive advantage comes from having a people advantage. One of the most impressive examples of a company affecting its bottom line through its people advantage is, again, Wal-Mart. To Sam Walton, the most important ingredient in Wal-Mart's success was the way it treated its associates, as he called his employees. He believed that if you want your staff to take care of the customers, you have to make sure you take care of the staff. Wal-Mart successfully created an environment where workers can offer their ideas and be listened to. It is no wonder that it has been recognized as one of the best companies to work for in the United States.

Wal-Mart creates value for its employees through responsibility and recognition, and delivers it through profit-sharing, in which 80 percent of employees participate. There is an ambitious company stock option program which by 1990 represented $1.8 billion in employee-owned equity, as well as other ongoing incentives. As you can see, Wal-Mart has created an environment in which the worker is as important as the shareholder and the customer. Consider the experience of employees at Wal-Mart's store in Mansfield, Ohio. There, a former store manager told an interviewer that communication is "one of Wal-Mart's strongest aspects [...] we share so much with each other through daily meetings, district meetings [and] satellite broadcasts."[5] The ordinary employees are party to decisions on sales, profits, inventory and markdowns.

The company solicits and rewards employee's ideas, encouraging initiative and creativity. In the "Yes We Can, Sam" suggestion program in 1993, associates came up with more than 650 ways to simplify, improve or eliminate work that resulted in estimated savings of more than $85 million. Tammy, a Mansfield associate says, "When we have an idea for improving the company we talk to the manager in charge of our area [...] If he thinks it's a good idea he talks to the store manager and backs us up on it."

Employees are empowered to take charge of their areas. "You get to do your job the way you want it to be done, taking care of people," says Tammy.

"We get to use our heads, and they let us run our own area." A colleague, Mike adds: "I know what needs to be done. If there is a piece of tile missing from the floor, I fix it. If the light bulbs are burned out, I replace them." This is a far cry from what happens at some other retailers where customer and employee value are not key management concerns.

Employees who don't feel a stake in the stores' success are unlikely to care about ensuring that merchandise is well organized and customers are made to feel important. It's axiomatic in retailing that poor employee morale opens a company to increased shoplifting since workers are less vigilant. As the business courses downward, employee unhappiness compounds the troubles.

Two other companies serve as successful examples of how employees are the key to enterprise value. One is Microsoft. Its founders and employees have generated more than $85 billion in market value by fully leveraging their intellectual capital. In his book on intellectual capital, Thomas Stewart asserts that Microsoft was incorporated for just this reason – to exploit intellectual capital through employee ownership.[6] The other is Barrick Gold, the large Canadian mining company. Barrick also realizes the important connection between people and shareholders. Its annual report cites these key performance objectives: developing full potential and entrepreneurial spirit in its employees and linking its employees with the interests of shareholders.

Shareholders

The third stakeholder in a company, the shareholder, expects a reasonable return on an investment over the long term. In turn, if the company meets shareholders' expectations for a reasonable rate of return, it will continue to enjoy access to capital. When that happens, shareholder value is created. But if a firm is not using its capital as successfully as other companies and is not showing much promise of doing so in the future, shareholders will pull their money out. The stock's value will drop, taking with it access to future capital and possibly the company's viability.

Again, Wal-Mart serves as an excellent example. The competitive advantage it has gained through providing both customers and employees with value resulted in increased market share and ultimately, value for shareholders through a higher share price and dividends. As shown previously in Figure 2.4, Wal-Mart's stock gave a 19,807 percent return between 1972 and 1992 not withstanding some recent growth related challenges.

Why isn't Wal-Mart's relationship with customers and employees self evident at every company? Because the contribution to value that each constituency makes only becomes obvious over a long period of time. Stakeholders' roles are not just linked for a profitable quarter or a record year of earnings. It is the positive result of a long-term perspective that enables a company to achieve that linkage. Understanding this is critical to effectively managing for value.

Dell Computer Corporation is another company that generates huge value for its shareholders in what is increasingly seen as a commodity business. In 1996, the stock quadrupled in value after a 71 percent unit sales growth and a 47 percent increase in revenues. Dell's success is largely the result of focusing on a key value attribute: speed. This attribute has become ingrained in the corporate culture, generating rapid improvements in how the business is run. A *BusinessWeek* article reported that one of the keys to this success was "educating people about return on capital and convincing them they could affect the future of the company."[7]

THE CASE FOR ENTERPRISE VALUE

To appreciate enterprise value the true long-term value of the organization must be recognized. Once it is acknowledged that value is long term it is obvious that it has to be created for each of the three key stakeholders. Customers are often looking for a long-term supplier who consistently provides quality products and services rather than having to constantly search for new sources. Employees generally prefer a stable relationship that is financially rewarding and challenging to moving from job to job. But the most graphic way to demonstrate value in the long term, is to look at it from a shareholder's perspective.

Too many executives believe that what shareholders really want is short-term increases in financial results that fire up stock prices. While it is true that share price does fluctuate with quarterly results, this occurs because shareholders often perceive these results to be indicative of future performance. Most analysts use short-term projections as a base for estimating future cash flows. If the short-term result is less than the projection, the most significant effect is on future projections, not simply the short-term result. To better understand this perspective, let's take a deeper look at shareholder value.

Shareholder value is commonly defined as return on investment or total shareholder return (TSR), made up of dividends plus share price appreciation. What drives dividends and share price appreciation is surplus cash flow or economic profit. We all know that a company's ability to pay dividends is directly related to its ability to generate surplus cash. But the force that drives share price appreciation is less obvious to many investors, even though it's the same thing. The difference is in the length of time. A company's ability to pay quarterly dividends depends on surplus cash. But a company's ability to drive up share price depends on its ability to consistently generate surplus cash well into the future. To understand the relevance of this fully, let's look at what determines share price.

Suppose that the current price of your shares is P_0, that the expected price at the end of a year is P_1, and that the expected dividend per share is DIV. The rate of return that investors expect over the next year is DIV plus the expected price appreciation per share P_1 minus P_0, all divided by the price at the start of the year P_0:

$$\text{Expected return (r)} = \frac{\text{DIV} + P_1 - P_0 - 1}{P_0}$$

If you are given investor forecasts of dividend and price and the expected return offered by other equally risky stocks, you can prove the validity of today's price:

$$\text{Price } (P_0) = \frac{\text{DIV} + P_1}{1 + r}$$

But what determines next year's price? While future stock prices are not easy to forecast directly, we can assume that if our price formula holds today, it will hold for future calculations as well. A year from now investors will be looking at dividends in Year Two and price at the end of Year Two:

$$P_1 = \frac{DIV + P_2}{1+r}$$

You can see the relation between today's share price and the forecast dividends for two years, plus the forecast price at the end of the second year. You could, of course, go on to the third year and on into the future as far as you like.

$$P_0 = \frac{DIV_1 + DIV_2 + DIV_n + P_n}{(1+r) \quad (1+r)^2 \quad (1+r)^n}$$

This gives us a "general stock price formula." The expression simply means that share price equals the present value of all dividends into the future.

The formula shows that share price is clearly a function of expected future dividends. Figure 2.5 shows much of a company's value comes in the distant future. We see that the present value of the dividend to be paid over the next five years amounts to an average of only 11.5 percent of current share price. Shareholders expect almost 90 percent of the value of their investment to come from the dividends a company will pay beyond five years. In other words, gains for investors are small for the first several years. Any significant value increases are many years away.

Because share price is a function of expected future dividends we know that the value of a business can only be fully realized over the long term. A company's ability to pay future dividends comes from its ability to generate future surplus cash flow. Consequently share price is driven by the company's ability to generate that surplus cash over the long term. Sustaining surplus cash flow into the future is only possible if you are able to sustain superior customer value into the future. Customer and shareholder value cannot be sustained unless the company also creates employee value over the long term. That is why the stakeholders in the company must be inextricably linked to accomplish and sustain value creation.

Figure 2.5   Share Price Relative to the Present Value of Expected Dividends Over the Next Five Years

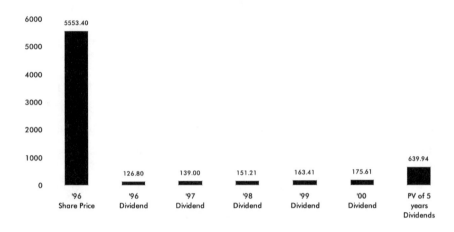

So a shareholder's perspective is a very long term one, extending over decades perhaps. But how do we reconcile the shareholder's long-term perspective with moment to moment share price volatility? Daily fluctuations would seem to run counter to everything that has been said. The answer to why share price is volatile is precisely because it is so long term. Small changes in a company's prospects have huge ramifications over time when projected over very long periods of time. The Minneapolis business column referred to earlier is an excellent illustration of this. It expected that workers' wages should increase when stock prices did. But tying wages to annual gains and losses is dangerous. If gains are passed on to workers in any given year, then likewise, losses should be too. We only need to refer to the market crash of 1987 to understand the point. In that year of historic losses, wages remained relatively stable. Why? Because the fluctuation then, as now, was just a small window in the long life of a stock.

Short-term fluctuations are generally affected by two things: external factors such as interest rates and inflation, and internal factors such as events within the company itself. For example, when there is bad economic news and a stock rises, it is usually concluded that it is owing to a function of the individual company's prospects, such as its growth rate, margins or investment intensity. The fluctuations caused by the prospects, amplified over time, have impact. The following examples illustrate this point.

In 1997, ABC Widget's revenues are projected to grow at 2 percent a year. The capital invested to sustain the business is equal to annual revenue and will be sustained at that level in the future. After-tax cash flows generated by the business are 20 percent of revenue. The projected net cash flows over the next year is shown below in Figure 2.6. The present value of this cash-flow stream, given a risk-adjusted cost of capital of 10 percent, would be $216.30.

When the growth rate is adjusted by a mere 1 percent: there is a 6 percent increase in the value of the cash flow as shown on the next page in Figure 2.7.

When the after-tax cash-flow margin is improved by 1 percent a 5.5 percent increase in value will be realized as show on the next page in Figure 2.8.

Thus you can appreciate that even small changes in the prospects for a business, compounded over time, ultimately have significant impact on share price, or value. As a result, you see constant fluctuations in share prices.

Figure 2.6   Base Case

ABC Widget: Base Case

Annual revenue growth	2%	Initial Investment Intensity	100%
After tax operating margin	20%	Investment intensity going forward	100%

Year	1	2	3	4	5	6	7	8	9	10	36	37	38	39	40
Revenue	100	102	104	106	108	110	113	115	117	120	200	204	208	212	216
Invested capital	100	102	104	106	108	110	113	115	117	120	200	204	208	212	216
After tax operating cash	20	20	21	21	22	22	23	23	23	24	40	41	42	42	43
Change in Invested Capital	0	2	2	2.1	2.1	2.2	2.2	2.3	2.3	2.3	3.9	4	4.1	4.2	4.2
Net cash flow	20	18	19	19	20	20	20	21	21	22	36	37	38	38	39

Present value of $216.3
Net cash flow

Figure 2.7   The Impact of Growth

Growth goes from 2% to 3%

Annual revenue growth	3%	Initial Investment Intensity	100%	
After tax operating margin	20%	Investment intensity going forward	100%	

Year	1	2	3	4	5	6	7	8	9	10	36	37	38	39	40
Revenue	100	103	106	109	113	116	119	123	127	130	281	290	299	307	317
Invested capital	100	103	106	109	113	116	119	123	127	130	281	290	299	307	317
After tax operating cash	20	21	21	22	23	23	24	25	25	26	56	58	60	61	63
Change in Invested Capital	0	3	3.1	3.2	3.3	3.4	3.5	3.6	3.7	3.8	8.2	8.4	8.7	9	9.2
Net cash flow	20	18	18	19	19	20	20	21	22	22	48	50	51	53	54
Present value of Net cash flow	$229.2														
Difference	$12.9	6.0%													

Figure 2.8   The Impact of Margin Improvement

Margin improves from 20% to 21%

Annual revenue growth	2%	Initial Investment Intensity	100%	
After tax operating margin	21%	Investment intensity going forward	100%	

Year	1	2	3	4	5	6	7	8	9	10	36	37	38	39	40
Revenue	100	102	104	106	108	110	113	115	117	120	200	204	208	212	216
Invested capital	100	102	104	106	108	110	113	115	117	120	200	204	208	212	216
After tax operating cash	21	21	22	22	23	23	24	24	25	25	42	43	44	45	45
Change in Invested Capital	0	2	2	2.1	2.1	2.2	2.2	2.3	2.3	2.3	3.9	4	4.1	4.2	4.2
Net cash flow	21	19	20	20	21	21	21	22	22	23	38	39	40	40	41
Present value of Net cash flow	$228.2														
Difference between scenarios	$11.9	5.5%													

Shareholders aren't the only ones who take a long-term view of a company. Seldom do regular, full-time employees take a new job with the intention of leaving soon. They generally hope that they will have a positive, long-term association with the firm. One of the biggest laments of life in the 90s, is that very few workers are collecting gold watches at retirement, as their parents and grandparents did. Employees desire a long-term engagement. As long as they continue to learn and grow in an environment that is satisfying, they will continue to derive value and will be reluctant to leave.

We know that customers see value in the long term too, evidenced by their loyalty. Wouldn't we all rather buy a car, a television or a refrigerator from a dealer who has been in business many years? That way we know the company will be there with warranty, parts and service. We can also point to advertising that touts how long a company has been in business, like "Tenth Anniversary Sale" or "Trusted Experience Since 1958." Companies know that longevity means consumer confidence. Organizations such as McDonald's proudly display the "Billions and Billions Served" sign at every store as evidence of the long-term consistency and value they provide to their customers. Business growth is very long term, regardless of which stakeholder perspective is taken.

Creating value for all is a necessary element of long-term success. For employees and customers, creating value means your company will be able to sustain research and development leading to new and improved products and services for customers, which ultimately means better value. For employees, economic profit can be invested in training and helping them acquire new skills or used to provide them with bonuses or share purchases.

And what about the shareholders? What would they like the company to do with value that has been created? It might seem that paying it out in the form of dividends would be the overriding preference. But, as we've seen so far, shareholders do look to the future for company growth. Shareholders prefer to have the company reinvest any surplus cash in initiatives that will generate better future returns. If the company can't think of any value-creating ways to use economic profit, then shareholders indeed want it back in dividends. But their general preference is to have it reinvested in value-creating growth.

To this point, only two of the top 100 Standard & Poor's companies pay more than 75 percent of their earnings in dividends. In fact, 80 percent of the S&P 100 pay less than half their earnings in dividends, while 40 percent of them paid less than a quarter. Even these very mature companies continue to reinvest profits in future endeavors. Managing for economic profit is managing for value, both current and future. The more economic profit a company generates, the more it can be investing in value-creating opportunities, a goal which ultimately serves all stakeholders. But practically, how does a company do this? Here is where the real challenge of balancing constituencies reveals itself.

One of the best pieces of evidence of the truth of enterprise value is the *FORTUNE* magazine study of the most and least admired companies. The correlation it looks for among the most admired is a link between customer satisfaction, employee satisfaction and high market share. In other words, it looks for the satisfying of stakeholder interests. The *FORTUNE* list is so credible because the criteria for it were developed from the perspective of all three stakeholders as illustrated in Figure 2.9.

Those companies that make it to *FORTUNE*'s annual list, as illustrated in Figure 2.10, are further proof that the equal focus of customer, employee and shareholder interests is one of the most compelling attributes a company can have.

Figure 2.9   Fortune Survey: What it Takes to be a Winner

- Quality of management
- Quality of product or services
- Innovativeness
- Community or environmental responsibility
- Ability to attract, develop and keep talented people
- Financial soundness
- Value as a long-term investment
- Use of corporate assets

Figure 2.10   Fortune Survey: America's Most Admired Companies

America's Most Admired Corporations
- Coca-Cola
- Mirage Resorts
- Merck
- UPS
- Microsoft
- Johnson & Johnson
- Intel
- Pfizer
- Procter & Gamble
- Berkshire Hathaway

Source: *FORTUNE*, March 3, 1997. Copyright © 1997, Time Inc.
All rights reserved. Reprinted by permission.

Creating enterprise value, value for all key stakeholders, is challenging. In fact, it is among the most demanding goals a company can set for itself because it requires that all levels of the business be run optimally. But the reasons to pursue it are significant. From an employee perspective, there is a strong correlation between maintaining a people advantage and competitive advantage. From a customer perspective, there's an important link between customer value and increased market share. And in both of those pursuits, the needs of shareholders are met by providing an outstanding financial return. Of course, there is no permanent state of grace even for successful companies; they must continually rebalance themselves and adjust to changes and challenges, even the challenges of success. When a company operates from a framework focused on value, such as Wal-Mart has, it provides a base for relevant cash-flow decisions that successfully balance the company's day-to-day interests with those over the long term. That is value-based management.

Chapter 3

MAKING VALUE YOUR MISSION
Reinventing Corporate Culture

Most companies today have mission statements that are meant to be fine expressions of their goals, but usually are a foggy mix of philosophy and action. But what senior management lays out in the mission statement is too often unattainable, because they have saddled themselves with the wrong kind of day-to-day corporate culture. This results in a big difference between what management says it will do and what it actually ends up doing. It is critically important to focus a company's corporate culture on creating value for all stakeholders. Creating value for all constituencies must be the company's mission, and if value is the mission, then it must also be the company culture, something that everyone, employees, customers and shareholders, understands and rallies around.

The word "value" often crops up in corporate mission statements, usually in reference to shareholder value. It's a popular thing to emphasize. But in reality, many companies fail to deliver. That's because in a truly value-driven company, the inextricable links between customers, employees and shareholders must be articulated in the mission statement. So the first step is to redefine the mission statement with respect to all three groups, to reflect the new value dynamics. Value must be the mission; it must become the primary management driver in the enterprise.

As with people, no two companies are alike, and so every firm must create its own unique solution to making value a key element of its culture. It is important to articulate the value for all stakeholders in the mission statement and, ultimately, in the company's deeds. Consider the following three examples of companies doing superior jobs of living the value culture for employees, customers and shareholders.

Microsoft is a company that creates strong value for its employees. It has declared that a relaxed, creative atmosphere is an important part of its culture. The corporate offices resemble a university campus. Employees have considerable freedom to design their work spaces in ways that suit their needs and work habits, with the overall goal of a casual environment that promotes innovative, creative thinking. There is a courtyard on the property with a stream and several waterfalls, where employees hold rubber duck races. Its cafeteria looks more like a ski-lodge restaurant than a corporate dining hall. Microsoft's commitment goes beyond the decor. It encourages all employees to think about creating value. When the company's worldwide retail-industry manager, Graham Clark, suggested that the company market its enterprise-wide architecture strategy to the retail industry, he sent a copy to Bill Gates. Only a week later, he got a reply, which simply said, "Go do it." As Andrea Umbach-Tevlin, Microsoft's manager of executive and management development says, "The people who do the grunt work around here are gold, and are to be treated as such."[1]

Lexus is an example of the customer service culture that creates customer value. It views its customers' experience as not just relating to the car but to the whole company. There are legendary stories about how people have found themselves far from home with their keys locked in their car. The Lexus response was, break the window and then visit the nearest Lexus dealer at your convenience and we'll replace it free. In another instance, new keys were hand delivered to a Lexus owner at no charge. Clearly, Lexus is a company that goes to extraordinary lengths to live the culture of customer service. It is a key part of their company culture and it has paid off handsomely by their being rated the No. 1 car company in customer service by J.D. Power and Associates for several consecutive years.

When it comes to living the culture of creating shareholder value we can't think of a better example than Berkshire Hathaway, operated by Warren Buffet. Annual meetings at Berkshire Hathaway are so enlightening that some people will buy a single share in the company just to attend. The attraction is Buffet's utter candor and commonsense approach to running a business. His philosophy is one of extraordinary openness toward shareholders. He recognizes that employees and customers, unlike shareholders, have far more information on which to base their day-to-day decisions. Shareholders do not enjoy that luxury. They invest their money and then trust the company to be good stewards of their investment. Investors have limited vehicles for communicating with the company. Buffet recognizes that shareholders have limited access to information, so he runs the company accordingly. Buffet spends a considerable amount of his time thinking about what shareholders need to know so that it can be communicated to them throughout the year, not just in the annual report. This is in stark contrast to the vague, glossed-over annual reports that are very often the only means of communication that companies have with their shareholders.

These three companies do a superior job of living the culture of value for customers, value for employees, and value for shareholders. The optimum goal, of course, is to pursue each one with the zeal that these companies have. While it may not always be possible in every organization, at the very least, a company must seek out and understand the inextricable links that exist in its corporate culture, and then find value creation for all three in order to create true enterprise value.

The Continental Airlines Story

The airline industry is not like most businesses. The life of airlines is far more rollicking, daring and mercurial than most other enterprises. The industry's standard accounting practices allow for debt levels that would make executives in other more conservative enterprises blanch. But it is still a business, one that needs to turn a profit, pay its bills, nurture its employees and protect its reputation. Some have done spectacularly well, only to wither and die – in the United States, Pan Am and PeopleExpress; in Britain, Laker Airways. Only a few have gone to the very brink and returned. Continental Airlines was one such company. It is a story of a great company with a splendid legacy that made a triumphant revival through intelligent focus on what really drives the success of the organization. And while it is said that the airline industry is not like most, Continental's vivid story of decline and stellar return to form is inspiring and instructive for managers in all enterprises on how value is created and destroyed.

Continental's greatness began in 1936 when a high-school dropout turned businessman, Robert Six, bought a stake in the pioneering carrier Varney Speed Lines for $90,000. Varney used Lockheed Vegas to carry mail between El Paso and Denver. Six renamed the carrier Continental in 1937, and began a reign that stressed quality service, an important lure for a public wary of the cost and hazards of early flying. It was the first US airline to serve hot meals and laid on champagne and brandy for first-class fliers. Before and after the Second World War, Six expanded the carrier's routes in Texas and the mountain states and modernized its fleet. The airline cultivated its reputation with the most profitable and frequent passenger, the businessperson, attending to her with comfort, amenities and quality. In turn, customers associated Continental as a high-end service, so its choice of the color gold for its tail was appropriate.

Customer value was not the only preoccupation for Robert Six. He liked to say that since he and his wife had no children he found fulfillment guiding his employees' careers. The camaraderie in the airline was such that at a time when other airlines faced unionization, Continental fleet and passenger-service employees rebuffed union drives. Employees made their careers at Continental and stayed, rather than hop to other companies, a telling indicator of the value they found in working for Six. Annual attrition rate among flight attendants in the early 1960s was below 3 percent.

Most major carriers fared well in the three decades after the Second World War when new technology and affluence brought a massive new market to airlines. But Continental was particularly rewarded thanks to superior customer and employee value. That in turn provided shareholders with incredible returns. The airline's revenue quadrupled every decade from $46 million in 1958 to $775 million 20 years later. Continental enjoyed one of the highest profit margins in an industry notorious for cyclical swings. Before the deregulation of the American airline industry in 1979, it posted a postwar net loss just twice, in 1958 and 1975. Continental's shares were the darling of institutional investors, who held 30.7 percent of its stock. Individual investors with small holdings kept them for years, such was their loyalty to Continental management.

Then, two developments changed everything. The first was deregulation. Continental had an old-style spiderweb of long-haul routes that crisscrossed the United States and received traffic from smaller regional airlines. After deregulation it lost its reliable supply of regional passenger feeds and found its spiderweb obsolete. Other airlines were fast switching to the hub-and-spoke system that fed passengers into central airports and gave them a plethora of convenient connections. Continental was suddenly squeezed by giant trunk carriers such as American and United as well as the regional airlines. Then, in June 1979, an American Airlines DC-10 crashed at Chicago's O'Hare airport, killing 272 people. The Federal Aviation Administration (FAA) grounded all domestic DC-10s pending investigation of their engine mounts. Continental had invested heavily in that plane and suddenly found 42 percent of its flying capacity confined to the tarmac. The DC-10 was later vindicated and quickly returned to service, but public confidence was slower to respond. Many consciously avoided it for months and even years afterward.

After four decades of building quality for customers, employees and shareholders, Continental began a long slide. It redrafted its route system around hubs in Denver and Houston and pursued a merger with Western Airlines in 1979 and 1981. The merger would reduce costs by combining stations and consolidating maintenance and eliminating route duplication. Continental management figured it could yield benefits of $91 million a year. They wanted to merge with another quality carrier and Western was the best candidate. But the Civil Aeronautical Board (CAB) blocked the first attempt and stalled the second.

By 1988 Continental was seen as one of the lowest quality airlines in the United States. It was first in passenger complaints to the US Department of Transportation (DOT) and the FAA cited it for poor safety stemming from years of obsession with cost cutting. Debt and poor customer and employee relations forced Continental into bankruptcy in December 1990. The fifth largest domestic carrier was saddled with too much debt.

In 1993, the new CEO, Robert R. Ferguson III brought in a special low-fare service on many short-haul routes in the east and called the program CALite. It undercut competitors by 50 to 80 percent and there were plans to double the program's size by 1994. The program focused on low costs, not good employee relations. CALite planes and their dispirited crews flew back and forth across the US, providing low-cost, low-quality service that in the end proved unsuccessful. By 1995 it faced a third liquidity crisis.

Then it began to turn around. Gordon Bethune was installed as CEO. He had served as president and COO and had a clear idea about creating value. He returned Continental to its beginnings, the kind of airline that Robert Six had established six decades before. His strategy was simple. "We had to put cheese back on the pizza. We have to do the things our customers value,"[2] he said. He added that employees would have a say in the operation, something that had been denied them since the late 1970s. The airline opened toll-free telephone numbers for employees to call about anything that needed improving. If, say, a flight attendant saw a broken seat on a plane, he or she could call in and the company committed itself to fixing the problem as quickly as possible. In the case of a broken seat, repair crews at the nearest station could be dispatched at once. Manning the phones were airline employees who understood the jargon and conditions callers spoke of. If a problem couldn't be fixed immediately, the airline promised employees it would have an answer within 48 hours. Suddenly, Continental airlines employees found they were being listened to again.

And the cost cutting came to an end. Although Continental continued to pare non-value-added costs, the days of lawn mowing every budget were over. Larry Kellner, chief financial officer, told an interviewer, "We don't just tell everybody to take 10 percent out of their budget."[3] Instead of blindly clipping reservation staff, it began to look at what effect staff cuts would have on business. Longer waits for a reservation agent resulted in potential passengers hanging up and taking their money elsewhere. In the end, Continental added staff to cut the wait and increase revenue. Bethune also shut down the CALite program and restored first-class service on many routes. Frequent fliers, who had looked to first-class passage as part of the reward for their loyalty, began to return, boosting Continental's share of the important business-flier market. And it meant a personal touch in dealing with passengers. Continental officials went out of their way to contact each irate customer and gave many of them first-class upgrades. Bethune himself personally courted top customers and the company continues to do so. "We had a crappy product and we were trying to discount ourselves into profitability," Bethune said. "Nobody wants to eat a crummy pizza, no matter if it is 99 cents."[4]

The turnaround was quick to come. *Frequent Flier* magazine and J.D. Power & Associates conducted a survey that found Continental first in customer-satisfaction among trunk-line carriers. It went from the back of the pack for DOT ratings to first place. Continental was also back in the black. It reported a profit of $224 million for 1995, reversing a $166 million loss the previous year. With characteristic grace, Bethune placed credit, and $50 million in performance bonuses, at the feet of his 35,000 employees. In the end, Continental learned the hard way that trading short-term profitability through cost cuts for things customers care about spells disaster. They learned the hard way that listening to customers and taking care of employees have never been more crucial. Bethune candidly told BusinessWeek: "You can't take your girlfriend for granted and you can't take your customer for granted [...] Somebody else gets them."[5]

Implementing a Value Program

Putting a value plan to work in a company is tough. Any rigorous change is slow and never happens overnight. Many organizations simply *declare* a value program into existence and expect the corporate culture to adapt to it. Often, they don't even have an understanding of their existing culture. It must be understood that a comprehensive cultural change first requires a keen understanding of the existing culture.

Creating a mission statement which emphasizes value is not enough. There are several useful techniques to begin to build the necessary imperative for change:

- Assessing Cultural Readiness
- Creating a Value Imperative
- Creating Leadership Alignment

ASSESSING CULTURAL READINESS

A cultural readiness assessment will establish a company's propensity for change and identify the unifying processes of the company. Since every organization uses a different process as its key management lever, each must find its own lever and work with it to put value creating in place. For example, during a recent consultation, one company keenly recognized that budgeting was a time-consuming endeavor, but that it also developed the social bond between managers and the organization. They viewed it as the crucial process. Consequently, any value program had to change the culture while recognizing the importance of budgeting and working with it. At another company, production management was of central importance, therefore production planning was key. Every company must begin at a designated critical leverage point that is particular to that firm. By focusing on making value changes to that process first, it is more likely to gain company-wide acceptance. The key is making an assessment of the existing culture. The more familiar the company is with its dynamics, the easier implementation of a new value culture will be.

A cultural assessment will determine an organization's readiness for change and locate the key leverage points that will help make those changes. The strengths and weaknesses of the existing culture and the readiness for making value the mission must be recognized; this may not necessarily mean making changes. Once it has been decided what works and where the obstacles are, the process can then move ahead selectively. Cultural change is difficult and not something that will happen by simple declaration. A logical path must be found where change will be embraced and make a big difference.

CREATING A VALUE IMPERATIVE

There are several ways to create a value imperative inside the organization, but there are a couple that have proven particularly useful. The first is the S curve, which plots the total shareholder return of the company compared with a group of its peers. For example, Figure 3.1 shows the returns of the

Figure 3.1   S & P 500 Five Year Total Return, December 1990-1995

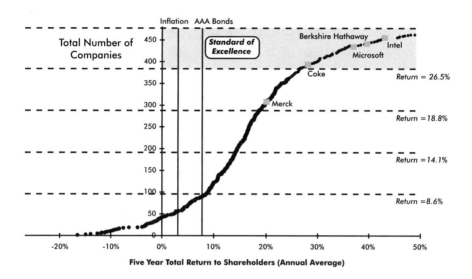

Source: Compustat, Braxton Analysis
    © 1996 Deloitte & Touche Consulting Group Braxton Associates

S&P 500 over five years. The client organization is compared with a group of their competitors in order to highlight its position. When the organization is at the top, the company wants to stay there. When they are at the bottom, clearly they must do better. Interestingly, no one wants to be in the middle.

One Canadian company compared the return on its shares against those provided by a triple-A bond. It clearly illustrated that the return provided by the company was lower than that of a less risky form of investment. The CFO then presented this data to his finance group staff along with some of the key implications, the main one being the difficulty the company would have in raising capital if returns continued at such a low level. This presentation was one of the key defining moments in this company's decision to truly make value its mission.

Another common technique to make value the imperative is the growth-returns matrix. This technique compares businesses, or units within a business, in terms of returns generated relative to the cost of capital and the growth of the assets of the business. Figure 3.2 shows that units earning less than the cost of capital while growing assets are clearly destroying value. Earning more than the cost of capital and shrinking assets limits the potential value creation. This technique illustrates that various parts of the business may be in different positions and require different strategies and can benefit from a value-based analysis of the whole business.

Figure 3.2   Growth Returns Matrix

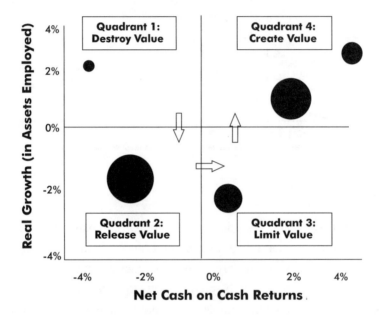

=$X in Aggregate Market Value

CREATING LEADERSHIP ALIGNMENT

Making value the mission requires a high level of management consensus as well as vocal and visible leadership. To begin to make this a reality it is best to begin with senior management sessions on the importance of value to the organization. These seminars make use of the companies' own data including

S curves and a growth-returns matrix to illustrate the performance of the company. These sessions are a necessary part of getting the management of the company to focus on a common direction. Using common change management techniques, the company then can begin to proceed on a Value Journey. In one company the seminar was so successful, that the organization immediately moved to adding cash flow to its key measures of performance changing its planning process to focus on value.

Clearly Continental Airlines' ticket to recovery came at a cost of hard lessons and tough cultural changes. Courageous decisions have restored the company to competitive prominence. The lesson is huge for anyone in business. The transition to a value enterprise is a process of change. The first step is the recognition of the need to change. The end goal is the creation of a true value proposition for customers, employees and shareholders. Only when a balance is achieved for all three, does a company prosper. The next step in our Value Journey is to explore how value can be assessed and measured in those three key areas.

Chapter 4

THE ENTERPRISE VALUE SCORECARD
Measure the Value Created

Let's look at a hypothetical example of a company with real life problems. While illustrative, the issues faced are common to many of our value implementation clients.

NationJet Airlines is doing just fine. It emerged from the turbulent era following airline deregulation as the dominant carrier in the overall market. It still enjoys a healthy 40 percent of the overall trade (on the routes it served), and in the lucrative premium business-travel market it commands a 65 percent market share. It is returning a profit, a gratifying result in the often spectacularly loss-ridden airline industry, and the company enjoys moderate if variable customer satisfaction. Some issues remain though. NationJet is yielding market share in the low-end travel market to its competitor, Budget Airways, and its share price is dropping. Management is not content to let these issues slip. Through strategic planning it has taken measures to fine tune the company and maintain its leadership. The problem is, NationJet is in big trouble. Management's tinkering is doing nothing to help and they won't realize it until it's too late.

There is no burning crisis that puts NationJet in the business press pages day after day, with stories questioning its long-term viability. NationJet is not fighting for its life, yet. Instead, there are creeping problems that will wear away at the airline's strength, adding to its costs, eroding customer service, sapping employee morale and delighting short-sellers on the stock market. Soon it will be in a grave crisis and NationJet's management will be scratching their heads over how, after all their vigilance, it came to be.

Enter George Braga, a new CEO, who suspects that something may be very wrong at NationJet, although it's far from clear exactly what. He will be a catalyst for change, but at other companies that person needn't be the CEO; agents of change can come from many levels of management. And while NationJet's particular crisis is an internal one, not every corporate problem is — some may be external. But Braga knows that change must occur.

After discussions with his management team and other NationJet employees Braga came to terms with the challenge. It would be difficult. There were a wide range of views on the issues and what the company should do about them. One thing was perfectly clear though — there was no consistent view as to why NationJet even existed in the first place. The CEO found the mission statement that had been developed several years earlier, which some employees still carried on printed plastic cards. It read: "We will provide the highest level of customer service while being the most cost-efficient airline in the industry and providing a satisfying place to work."

After more discussion at the management table it became clear that the statement was not being applied and, in fact, there were things which conflicted directly with it. Cost and service were continually in conflict and being traded off. And the ones who always suffered were the employees. George Braga decided he had heard enough. While a new mission statement itself would not solve the problem, it was time to chart a new course for NationJet. He knew it would be a long journey but a clear direction is a vital first step.

Braga started by consulting employees but he knew that overall direction must come from him. After trying and rejecting several ideas he kept coming back to the same issue. He expressed it in these words, "Our mission is to create value for all our key stakeholders including customers, employees and investors through continuous focus on delivering what they care about." With this as a starting point he began getting the organization focused on this goal. He knew that expressing the goal in terms of outcomes would be critical to moving forward because managers would have difficulty in letting go of the old metrics.

* * * * *

If you are wondering why you have never heard of NationJet Airlines, or the dynamic George Braga, it is because they do not exist outside the pages of this book. This is a fictitious airline created to illustrate aspects of the Value Journey. NationJet was created as an example to demonstrate how the Value Journey in a corporation begins and how it moves forward, gradually changing and focusing the operation on what really creates value for all stakeholders.

George Braga was coming to grips with what inputs he needed to take stock of the company. The first task any company must undertake if it is to deal firmly with enterprise value is to learn how to measure accurately the customer, employee and shareholder value a company generates. Very few companies do a good job of measuring enterprise value. All companies measure shareholder value – by law, they are required to prepare and file financial statements – but few companies employ *good* measures of shareholder value. Most still employ an earnings perspective of the business that suffers from several shortcomings. Only recently have companies discovered that a cash-flow perspective of the business provides a better measure of shareholder value.

The state of customer value is similar to that of shareholder value measurement. Many companies believe that they are measuring customer value by measuring customer satisfaction. Although customer satisfaction is an important component in understanding customer value, it is not the entire answer, and firms are discovering that they are losing *satisfied* customers. Companies such as AT&T have responded to this predicament by developing customer value analysis (CVA), a measurement we'll describe later in this chapter.

The state of employee value measurement is unlike that of customer and shareholder value. Very few companies bother to measure employee value. And when they do, they often simply look at the value of the employee to the company, not the value an employee realizes from his or her job. It's a two-way street. The value of an employee to a company is often a function of the value they realize from working at the company. In this chapter we will examine the current state of enterprise value measurement and explore new and better ways of measuring customer, employee and shareholder value.

Measuring Customer Value

All companies know whether they are creating value for their customers simply by watching their sales figures. Unfortunately, these reveal little about
how a company creates value for its customers and, therefore, provides the
company with little insight into how to manage the value it creates for customers. Information from customer satisfaction surveys can reveal something
about how a company creates value for its customers, but customer satisfaction information alone is not enough. Customer value is a function of both the
satisfaction with the quality of a product or service and its price. The quality
must provide some form of utility or enjoyment that is perceived to be worth
more than the price paid for the customer to realize value from the purchase.
In competitive markets, customers will choose the products or services that
offer the greatest value – the best combination of perceived quality and price.

Companies are often reluctant to measure customers' perceptions about
the quality of their product and/or service. They view customers' perceptions
as subjective and difficult to quantify. As Shlomo Maital, author of *Executive
Economics* points out:

> The subjective nature of value creation means that what truly creates value
> for customers remains something of a mystery. However, the language of
> economics insists that when choices are made, the value of options must
> be weighed against their price or cost. No decision can be made, unless
> our knowledge of values is at least as extensive and accurate as our under-
> standing of prices. The subjective nature of values is no excuse for not
> trying to estimate their magnitudes. … What people perceive and think is
> as important a part of reality as the physical quantities we regard as emi-
> nently real. With some effort, these perceptions, too, can be brought into
> relation with numbers. Good decisions depend on doing so. [1]

The first step in measuring customer value is to have a clear understanding of what customers care about. In generic terms this is easy. Customers
care about getting an appropriate level of quality for a reasonable price relative to the alternatives. At an aggregate level then, customer value can be
measured as follows:

$$\text{Customer Value} = \frac{\text{The Perceived Worth of the Offering}}{\text{The Perceived Worth of the Alternatives}}$$

A score greater than one should allow a firm to increase its market share, while a score of less than one would imply market share loss. The issue is still the same, however, what do customers really care about and what are they willing to pay for?

The traditional approach to determining what customers care about is what is commonly referred to as a customer-satisfaction index. In this approach customers are asked a series of questions about the product or service and a satisfaction index is created. However, this may not identify what customers really care about and, more importantly, what they are willing to pay for. In the case of AT&T, customers rated the service as high or better, but they were still defecting in large numbers. AT&T developed a new measurement that is now commonly known as customer value analysis (CVA). These are its key attributes:

- analysis of price-to-quality, not just quality or satisfaction
- a link to customer retention, growth and acquisition and, hence, revenue, demand and market share
- everything is relative to competitors' customer-value proposition

Customer value's origins are examined in Figure 4.1. In most industries the revenue line can be broken down from the income statement into price and volume (or units sold). Further deconstructing volume you measure overall demand for a product or service multiplied by market share. Customer value analysis (CVA) links factors of demand and price. It's possible to model

Figure 4.1   Modeling Customer Value

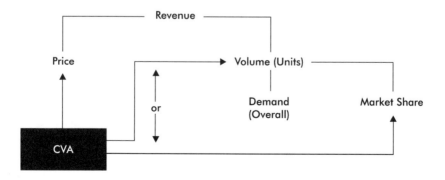

changes in demand and market share and even how well a proposed product will be accepted by the marketplace and what impact it will have on other products, including the company's own and those of its competitors.

Paul Dernier is one of the foremost experts in modeling customer value. His customer value models establish customer value as a function of price and perceived quality relative to competition. Customers buy value which is quality relative to price. Quality includes all non-price attributes. Quality can be broken down into two main areas: the quality of the product itself and the quality of service. It is worth noting that product quality has a lot to do with the suite of services provided with the product, such as, billing, installation, etc. In most true segment services the quality of the physical product may have limited importance to the overall value proposition to the customer.

Figure 4.2 breaks down customer-perceived quality in terms of its main attributes. For each of these, there will be subattributes (which may have their own sub-subattributes and so on). It's not strictly hierarchical; some attributes may share some common subattributes much like hyper-linked

Figure 4.2   Attributes of Customer Value

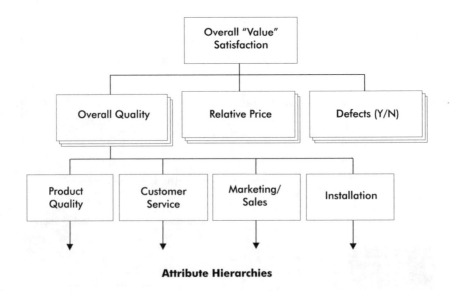

Attribute Hierarchies

World Wide Web pages. This breakdown of relative quality is discovered through market research. The quality and precision of the findings will only be as good as the quality and precision of the research. Another point is that there should probably be a set of these data for every product-market segment combination. If the company has five products and five market segments, it should have 25 product-market segments. This research can be costly. And this approach lends itself to products and services that are generally sold to consumers although it can be modified and adapted for use by companies selling to a small number of commercial or industrial customers. In these instances, each significant customer could be treated as a segment.

It helps to portray the findings from a customer value analysis using a customer value map as illustrated in Figure 4.3.

The map plots relative quality on the x axis and relative price on the y axis. Average relative price and quality become the center point for the map. A line running from the lower left corner to the upper right, to the

Figure 4.3   Customer Value Map

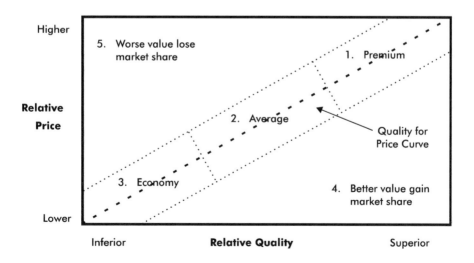

Source: Adapted from *Managing Customer Value* by Bradley T. Gale (New York: Free Press, 1994)

midpoint represents the trade-off consumers are willing to make between relative price and relative quality. If customers are very price sensitive we would expect the slope of the line to be flat. If customers are relatively price insensitive then they would pay relatively more for a small improvement in quality. So the objective is to be below the line. If a product or a service is below it, it is offering a superior price-quality combination and should expect to enjoy greater customer attention and customer acquisition. Note that it can be below the line with either inferior (or relatively inferior) quality or with relatively superior quality. It's really the combination of relative quality and relative price that dictates the value. Think of Southwest Airlines, the most successful of the US no-frills carriers with a combination of low amenities but also low price. The price is low enough to more than compensate for the lower quality in fliers' minds, enabling Southwest to capture market share.

The customer value map depicted in Figure 4.3 is divided into five sections. Section 1 represents the area of the map for premium products of higher price and quality. Section 3 is for economy products of lower price and quality. The second section represents "average" quality for price. Section 4 pertains to products with exceptional value, whereas products in Section 5 offer poor value. As long as a product is on the price-for-quality line, in which quality is appropriate for the price, customers will probably continue to buy. If a product is below the line, it will be winning over customers and, therefore, gaining market share. If it's above the line customers may begin to defect. This, of course, is influenced by factors such as loyalty that may allow a company to operate above the line for a time.

Now NationJet's CEO must get a handle on the company's customer attributes. NationJet's customer segregation has focused on its two strategic business units: passengers and cargo. In turn, the passenger unit is divided between business-class passengers and budget travelers. The airline has conducted extensive customer satisfaction surveys that showed NationJet enjoying generally strong customer satisfaction. With its customer value analysis it can dig deeper than the satisfaction studies. Value modeling takes this a step further by linking the activities performed to create customer value with their cost.

Two conclusions emerged from NationJet's CVA. The first was that for the business flier, NationJet had a huge dominance in market share and that would probably continue through its superior scheduling, in-flight amenities, roomy seats and its frequent-flier programs, despite some problems. But the picture with budget travelers was not so bright. Although cheap-fare fliers liked NationJet's service quality, they were defecting to rival Budget Airways which had markedly lower prices. The customers drift toward providers of the product or service characteristics they look for. Quality consumers will, for example, go to quality providers, while the impecunious will drift toward budget services.

Measuring Shareholder Value

In Chapters Two and Three we saw how total shareholder return is a function of expected future dividends, and that the best indicator of a company's ability to pay those, is its ability to generate cash flow. As investors see it, total shareholder return is the most important measure of corporate performance and the scorecard is cash flow. If a company's objective is to manage for value, a cash-flow approach in calculating performance makes a lot of sense. Unfortunately, many companies use another method that is less appropriate for measuring value creation — the traditional earnings approach. A vital tool in accounting, it serves a very useful purpose. It is based on certain overarching principles to guide business: relevance, reliability, neutrality, fidelity, verifiability, comparability, consistency and so forth. Accounting, by its nature, serves many masters, the corporation, its shareholders, regulators and suppliers. It provides a structure for tax reporting to governments and helps management to sum up its past activities. It should not, however, be pressed into measuring a company performance from a value perspective. But this is too often the case. Although an effective record of a company's past activities, it is insufficient to help see where it is going. Indeed, it can lead to decisions that actually destroy value for the company.

The earnings approach is useful in providing an accurate, ethical and impartial reflection of a company's existing and past value. It provides information that is useful to investors, creditors and others in making investment, credit, regulatory and other decisions. Reporting systems based on financial accounting models and generally accepted accounting principles provide valuable information to senior management regarding the operation of divisions, subsidiaries and other business units. It can monitor the performance of a company's management, and in turn those managers can assess their own performance and that of their employees.

The earnings approach generally calculates shareholder value with a straightforward and static concept, usually earnings or profit times some multiple, such as price to earnings. It adjusts the figures to make the last accounting year representative of future years, to provide fair representation of a company's financial position. Compare the earnings approach to a still photograph, a sharply rendered record of life taken in a fraction of a second but revealing little about the continuity of life. In order to make the static single snapshot representatives of the overall life of a corporation come alive, financial adjustments must be made to things such as depreciation, accounts receivable and payable, work-in-progress inventories and so on. Managers try to smooth out the picture, but like cartographers drawing maps of the globe, they create distortions. While it is sometimes important to smooth extraordinary items and events, such as plant closings, recurring decisions smoothed over a long period of time twist the company's portrait. As the cash-flow theorist Alfred Rappaport has written, "the problem lies not so much with accounting but rather its use by managers for unintended, inappropriate purposes. Accrual accounting conventions are governed by the objectives and institutional constraints of corporate reporting."[2]

By contrast, the cash-flow approach is what sophisticated investors rely on to judge a business's worth, and it is an approach that a company should be using to determine whether it is creating value. Its very name is synonymous with its goal, to measure the continuous flow of cash that a company has and is expected to generate. The cash-flow approach is fundamentally different from the traditional earnings perspective. The overriding assumption in the traditional approach is that a company's value can be forecast based on its reported earnings. The cash-flow perspective sees value as a function of expected future cash flows, which gives a broad, long-term picture of the company's value by considering cash flow, timing and risk.

It is instructive to think of a business in the way owners of corner stores do. The store owner has one thing on his mind, and it's not net income, depreciation or any other item in the earnings approach arsenal. It's cash. What's in the till at the end of the day is the owner's benchmark for how well his business is doing. If there's cash in the box, he knows he can open his doors next day. He will, of course, have his accountant prepare an income statement at the end of the year because tax authorities and bankers require it. But he knows the outcome even before he receives the statement. And so it should be with corporate managers. Cash flow is the economic pulse of any business or division, large or small, and should always be the leading tool managers use to guide their actions.

Cash flow is a purer measure of performance than other accounting-based indicators such as profit and earnings. For example, there are many extraneous things that affect stocks. When the market values a stock in the short term, external factors such as interest rates and inflation make it impossible for investors to understand exactly what caused the fluctuation. Is the daily share price they read in the paper a result of the company being managed well or poorly, or is it owing to fluctuations in interest rates, inflation or some combination of factors? Because it is impossible to separate a company's performance from the extraneous factors affecting its stock price in the short run, investors strive for a long-run, stable indicator that is a purer measure of a company's true performance. And cash flow is that measure.

Numerous students of the cash-flow approach bear out its value in reflecting a company's direction. Rappaport reintroduced the idea of cash flow as a business principle in his pioneering work *Creating Shareholder Value*, published in 1986. His study is considered one of the more significant recent contributions to modern strategic management. Subsequent studies bear out his important work. One study, performed by Braxton Associates, the strategy consulting arm of Deloitte & Touche Consulting Group, shows that cash-flow based returns are much more strongly correlated to share price than earnings per share measures, as shown on the next page in Figure 4.4.

The study compares the correlation between an accounting approach and share price, and a cash-flow approach and share price. It reflects hundreds of similar studies that always show the same result. Cash flow is a superior

Figure 4.4   A Clearer Picture: Why the Cash-Flow Approach Makes More Sense

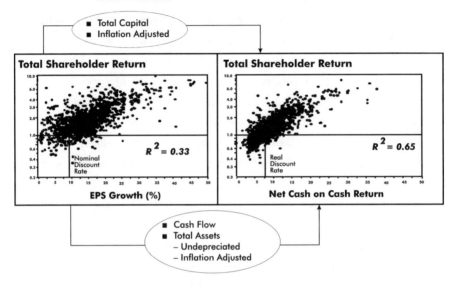

Source: Braxton Analysis
   © 1996 Deloitte & Touche Consulting Group Braxton Associates

measure of value as reflected in share price. This is what Boeing discovered when it was rethinking its financial performance metrics. In *Cash Flow and Performance Measurement: Managing for Value*, Harvey Davis of the Financial Executives Research Foundation writes:

> Boeing looked at correlation charts showing how well several different measures explained the share prices of publicly traded companies. It found a very low correlation between price-earnings ratios and earnings-per-share growth rates and only a slightly better correlation between the ratio of equity price to book value and ROE minus the cost of capital (calculated by the Capital Asset Pricing Model [CAPM]). There was a strong correlation between market price per share and predicted value per share based on analysts' published cash-flow forecasts. Boeing gathered evidence of the correlation of stock prices and long-term free cash flow prices from several sources. From this research, it was concluded that stock prices for Boeing and most other companies do indeed track cash-flow projections over longer periods, although there may be substantial volatility over shorter periods.[3]

Still, the cash-flow approach is a drastic departure from what most managers are accustomed to and what they trust in day-to-day operations. They have always been more comfortable with income numbers, annual earnings, return on investment and earnings per share as proxies for value. Income numbers are not only what managers are comfortable with, but they make up the very fabric of their intuition. A senior executive at a large Canadian company was a big advocate of its value program and thus, the cash-flow approach. He had learned a great deal about the value perspective and believed in it. In one of the strategic planning sessions, he kept insisting that the cash-flow numbers be reconciled back to the accounting perspective. He finally confessed that he was still having trouble converting things in his head from the new language of value back into the old accounting world. He likened the process to an adult learning a second language.

Why are companies so stuck in traditional accounting perspectives? First, history and custom have influenced the widespread use of traditional accounting. And, as Rappaport's cash-flow perspective has become more widely known and accepted over the last decade, it has really only been assimilated by the senior levels at most companies. A developed cash-flow sense at the operating levels still eludes most businesses. Even today, the liquidation model remains standard financial reporting. It is what managers know and they are comfortable with. No wonder it's still part of every business school curriculum around the world. It is also constantly reported in the business press in various forms. But as was discussed in Chapter Two, book value, or the liquidation model, rarely reflects a company's true value. Over the past five years, market values have consistently been greater than twice book value (Figure 4.5 illustrates this point).

Changes in the market's perception of value has been made evident in its abandonment of the price-to-book ratio that has been historically used as an indicator of whether the market is overvalued. Throughout the 1960s, the market backed off every time the ratio reached 2.25. Yet on November 21, 1996, the price-to-book ratio for the S&P 500 reached an all-time high of 4.23. It is obvious that analysts today do not place much value on this indicator because they understand that the economy and companies have fundamentally changed. This view is best expressed by

Figure 4.5   Market to Book Values

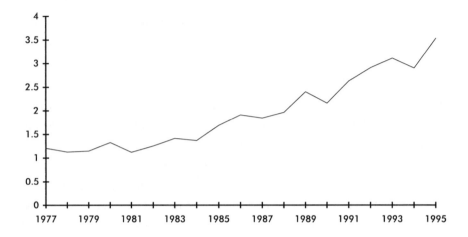

Source: Standard and Poor's

Alfred Goldman, director of market analysis at A.G. Edward & Sons Inc., who says, "We're getting away from rust bucket firms where everything is tied up in plant and equipment. Companies don't have to replace their capital every five years." [4]

How are cash-flow numbers really different from accounting numbers and how can they be made relevant to operating managers? What follows are three practical but hypothetical examples which, while simple, are accurate representations of the problems we frequently see in companies. Typically, these kinds of problems disguise themselves and are hard to uncover, but they are there. Most of them don't represent dysfunctional behavior so much as inadequate views of the world or incomplete understanding of the ramifications of activities throughout a company's units.

ACCOUNTS PAYABLE

Joe Smith is the purchasing manager for ABC Widget Company. He has just spent two grueling weeks negotiating with suppliers. He rose through the ranks of the company to become head of purchasing and receives a nice salary. The performance component of his salary centers on his ability to negotiate lower prices on the company's supplies. He knows that lower prices will reduce the company's cost of goods sold and go right to the net income line. Today, he is delighted and celebrating as a result of the last two weeks. He negotiated significant price reductions, as shown in the following table with lower cost of goods sold. However, there were changes in the payment terms. These won't have an obvious effect on net income, but will have an effect on value creation.

Think of accounts payable as equivalent to a loan from your suppliers. In this case, a lower raw materials price was negotiated but the supplier also reduced the terms of payment by 30 days. That means Smith's company must increase its working capital to get the bill paid on time. The value reduced by accelerated payables, more than wipes out the savings in supplies he was so delighted with. The net present value of the cash flow has changed from 4.55 to 4.18, an 8 percent reduction as shown on the next page in Figure 4.6. Did his victory and resulting increase in incentive compensation reward the shareholders? No. In fact, they took a hit — twice. Once because working capital had to be increased and again when they got the honor of paying for his compensation bonus even though value was destroyed.

ACCOUNTS RECEIVABLE

Mary Green is a sales manager with ABC Widgets. Considerable portions of the company's annual income rest on her ability to generate new customer and revenue growth. She has an aggressive compensation package based on her generating new business. After several successful years of growth, sales were stagnating. Green came up with a clever program that enabled her to penetrate the smaller end of the market, an area the company had never serviced. Since its implementation, sales orders indicate that ABC Widgets is growing significantly. But buried in the details of her plan are extended terms ideally suited for small, cash-strapped customers. From a traditional perspective, it looks like she is on track to make the President's Club and get her trip to Hawaii.

Figure 4.6   Impact of Purchase Price Reductions

	Base Year	Year 1	Year 2	Year 3	Year 4	Year 5	5 Year Cummul. Net Inc.	PV of Cash Flows
Existing Business Plan								
Income statement								
Revenue	12.00	12.00	12.00	12.00	12.00	12.00		
Cost of goods sold	10.80	10.80	10.80	10.80	10.80	10.80		
Net income	1.20	1.20	1.20	1.20	1.20	1.20	**6.00**	
Balance sheet								
A/P	1.80	1.80	1.80	1.80	1.80	1.80		
Cash flows		1.20	1.20	1.20	1.20	1.20		**4.55**

Lower cost of goods sold (Cost of goods sold goes from 90% of revenue to 89%. Payment terms go from 60 days to 30 days.)

	Base Year	Year 1	Year 2	Year 3	Year 4	Year 5	5 Year Cummul. Net Inc.	PV of Cash Flows
Income statement								
Revenue	12.00	12.00	12.00	12.00	12.00	12.00		
Cost of goods sold	10.80	10.68	10.68	10.68	10.68	10.68		
Net income	1.20	1.32	1.32	1.32	1.32	1.32	**6.60**	
Balance sheet								
A/P	1.80	0.89	0.89	0.89	0.89	0.89		
Cash flows		0.41	1.32	1.32	1.32	1.32		**4.18**

Accounts receivable went up and bad debts increased as a result of the new extended credit plan. Working capital had to be increased, erasing whatever benefits accrued from higher net income. As illustrated in Figure 4.7, there appeared to be an improvement from the accounting perspective — increased net income, but cash flow was being reduced by almost 40 percent, with the net present value going from 4.17 to 2.80. Thus, value had been destroyed. Shareholders once again got to give out a bonus for the privilege of losing value.

INVENTORIES

ABC Widgets has recently embarked on a total quality management program (TQM) which pleased some key customers. ABC had decided to court cus-

Figure 4.7   Accounts Receivable Example

	Base Year	Year 1	Year 2	Year 3	Year 4	Year 5	5 Year Cummul. Net Inc.	PV of Cash Flows
Existing Business Plan								
Income statement								
Revenue	12.00	12.00	12.00	12.00	12.00	12.00		
Cost of goods sold	10.80	10.80	10.80	10.80	10.80	10.80		
Bad debt	0.10	0.10	0.10	0.10	0.10	0.10		
Net income	1.10	1.10	1.10	1.10	1.10	1.10	**5.50**	
Balance sheet								
A/R	1.00	1.00	1.00	1.00	1.00	1.00		
Cash flows		1.10	1.10	1.10	1.10	1.10		**4.17**
Extended credit plan (Payment terms goes from 90 days to 60 days, bad debt goes from 10% of A/R to 15%)								
Income statement								
Revenue	12.00	14.40	17.28	20.74	24.88	29.86		
Cost of goods sold	10.80	12.96	15.55	18.66	22.39	26.87		
Bad debt	0.10	0.36	0.43	0.52	0.62	0.75		
Net income	1.10	1.08	1.30	1.56	1.87	2.24	**8.04**	
Balance sheet								
A/R	1.00	2.40	2.88	3.46	4.15	4.98		
Cash flows		-0.32	0.82	0.98	1.18	1.41		**2.80**

tomers with just-in-time (JIT) strategies, so they devised a program to become a preferred supplier. ABC's inventory managers learned that they needed to guarantee that for every 100 orders their customer gives them, they will deliver 99 as finished goods by the next day. This advantage allowed them to grow revenue at 5 percent a year at a time when industry growth was flat. Because they had yet to establish a complete system to anticipate, coordinate, and electronically receive orders, they had to supplement their finished goods inventory to ensure that 99 percent fulfillment rate. The benefit from the 5 percent revenue growth rate, however, will be more than offset by the rise in inventory. This TQM team had effectively generated new revenue in a stagnant market, and for that reason, they were commended for their creativity and innovative thinking in generating revenue. At a recent TQM seminar the team was awarded the "Team First" award for their stellar efforts.

Again, the additional working capital tied up in increased inventories more than offset the improvement in net income, so value was destroyed as shown in Figure 4.8. The net present value of cash flows dropped from 4.55 to 4.04, a reduction of more than 11 percent. Is it any wonder that shareholders seldom get overly excited when a company announces that they are moving toward Total Quality Management?

Clearly, it was not an intentional decision for the company to build up inventory, but it became a by-product of the larger goal of that 99 percent fulfillment rate. An accretion of small events in pursuit of a larger goal often destroys value. This hypothetical example often occurs in real life. The sales

Figure 4.8   Inventory Example

	Base Year	Year 1	Year 2	Year 3	Year 4	Year 5	5 Year Cummul. Net Inc.	PV of Cash Flows
Existing Business Plan								
Income statement								
Revenue	12.00	12.00	12.00	12.00	12.00	12.00		
Cost of goods sold	10.80	10.80	10.80	10.80	10.80	10.80		
Net income	1.20	1.20	1.20	1.20	1.20	1.20	**6.00**	
Balance sheet								
Inventories	0.90	0.90	0.90	0.90	0.90	0.90		
Cash flows		1.20	1.20	1.20	1.20	1.20		**4.55**
Reduced stock-outs plans (Inventory goes from 30 days to 60 days, Revenue growth goes from 0 to 5% per year.)								
Income statement								
Revenue	12.00	12.60	13.23	13.89	14.59	15.32		
Cost of goods sold	10.80	11.34	11.91	12.50	13.13	13.78		
Net income	1.20	1.26	1.32	1.39	1.46	1.53	**6.96**	
Balance sheet								
Inventories	0.90	1.89	1.98	2.08	2.19	2.30		
Cash flows		0.27	1.23	1.29	1.35	1.42		**4.04**

group of one of our clients sold a very large order based on better delivery. The production and delivery arms went to heroic efforts to meet the new capabilities. But they had to deal with certain preset constraints such as minimum production runs that were established to meet operational efficiency which, in turn, met the company's performance measurements. Then there were standard practices to consider, such as pushing ahead back orders. The result was that small piles of finished goods in inventory began to show up in several warehouse locations, on order expediters' desks, and in customer sites, and for very good reason. The production division was trying to serve two masters. The customer to which the sales team had made the commitment, and the company's traditional performance measurement system that was built around operational efficiency and delivering maximum accounting profits and earnings. The situation was not the child of dysfunctional behavior or an intentional value-destroying plan, but rather, a series of right decisions that cumulatively led to the wrong outcome. The company had a compartmentalized view of its activities and a poor understanding of cross organizational impacts.

The above examples illustrate problems that a cash-flow perspective can uncover. Many organizations are adept at trading off investment against improvement in operating expenses. Most do a poor job, however, of assessing how the investment will cross boundaries. A business unit must ask if an investment will optimize its process, its product and its part of the organization, and will there be cross-organizational impacts that are not readily evident and are not represented in that business case. But first, it is necessary to install the capabilities to track the information that will give the answers. While many capital-expenditure cases center on revenue stimulation, it is remarkably common for the organization never to track revenue once the expenditure is in place. Often it's because they are not capable of it. The goal has to be finding the trade-offs company-wide. And it can only happen when the company's framework is comprehensively cash-flow based.

Consider some numbers from a high-tech services company in Figure 4.9, which portray another excellent example of how traditional earnings numbers can differ dramatically from a cash-flow perspective.

When the accounting-based return on average common equity (RACE, a net income return), is graphed against cash-flow return on invested capital

Figure 4.9   Uncovering a Hidden Failure: The Cash-Flow vs. Traditional Accounting Method

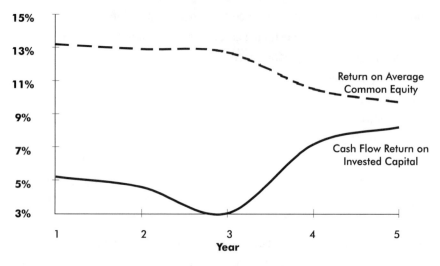

(CFROI), two very different stories emerge. The earnings perspective portrays a company that had acceptable investor returns through the first three years, including record earnings in the third year, followed by significant decline. But look what the cash-flow perspective reveals. The company has failed to meet investor expectations throughout the whole period. From a cash perspective, Year 3 was the company's worst year, with significant improvement in the last two years. Obviously, the manager relying on the accounting numbers will end up with a different conclusion than the one using cash-flow numbers.

The earnings approach comes up short when earnings and cash flow diverge. In the case of a company with relatively little or no capital, earnings can be a good proxy for cash flows. When we factor in for accounts payable and inventories, however, the two approaches provide contrasting results. PepsiCo has discovered that a cash-flow perspective has helped its people think in new ways. As Harvey Davis writes in *Cash Flow and Performance Measurement: Managing for Value:*

> The company is starting to refranchise its restaurants – selling them to franchisees — and believes that this move could pull more than $500 million out of the restaurant business without changing earnings at all.

One of PepsiCo's restaurant divisions is in the process of reconcepting and, with the success of this process, plans to add a number of new units. Historically, new capital has been required for new units. But PepsiCo has challenged the division to generate cash for the new units by refranchising existing units. That way the division gets a double win; it redeploys money from lower-return assets to higher-return assets.[5]

The question then becomes one of how to achieve a cash perspective in a world more familiar with the earnings approach.

Measuring Employee Value

When it comes to employee attributes, NationJet tends to limit its efforts to conducting annual employee reviews and exit interviews. Human Resources gives employees a questionnaire to fill out and return to their supervisors. The answers show broad worker satisfaction, and yet the airline has a history of employee unrest. Despite enjoying compensation packages that are at the industry norm, the unions representing pilots, cabin and ground crew and machinists have launched a series of tumultuous strikes. Through employee value analysis, NationJet came to the conclusion that satisfied employees don't necessarily mean cooperative employees. George Braga began to reflect on the importance of focusing on the value the company could create for employees relative to other airlines. As a result, he planned to replace the annual employee satisfaction questionnaire with quarterly employee focus groups and surveys. He also planned to survey employees in similar labor markets, such as the hospitality industry, to get an ideas of how NationJet compares.

While many companies are using the wrong measures for customer and shareholder value, they are at least attempting to measure the value they create for these stakeholders. When we talk to managers about people value, they invariably assume that we are talking about the value that employees contribute to the business. The concept of understanding and measuring the value that employees derive from their employment seems novel. Some managers today view this information as a potential lever to increase labor productivity, an idea which is not at all novel.

In the 1930s, research on productivity conducted at the Hawthorne Works of the Western Electric Company in Chicago led to the conclusion that productivity was directly related to the degree of group teamwork and cooperation among workers. The finding started a "human relations" movement which spent the next two decades researching and theorizing about the concept that group behavior and workers' feelings were associated with morale and productivity. The concept was nicknamed the Pet Milk Theory after the Pet Milk Company, which boasted in ads that its product was superior because it came from contented cows. This bovine satisfaction was similar to the notion that happy workers are more productive. Accordingly, proponents implemented company picnics, staff awards and rewards, employee coffee rooms and other gimmicks. But failure to find any proof that such ideas boosted workers' satisfaction, and therefore productivity sent this idea to an early grave. Too many companies thought they could manipulate employees to boost their output. What they needed to do was to look at a longer term with more fundamental improvements to both employee fulfillment and benefits to the company.

But in the last ten years business has renewed its interest in quality of work life, not because it has become sentimental or altruistic, but because corporations face a crisis in productivity. Many Western businesses have studied Japanese management techniques with their high levels of employee participation in decision making and their focus on group consensus. Some businesses have begun adopting these techniques to reverse the stagnation in employee productivity. But if companies were to adopt the enterprise perspective to value, then they would not think of people value as merely a lever to manipulate productivity. They would aspire to create value for people as one of the critical goals of the enterprise.

Very few companies measure the value they create for their employees. Those that do use variations of an system known as People Value Management (PVM). This is a system that measures the value that a company generates for its employees. It is also relative to the value proposition offered by rival employers and determines the extent to which a company can retain and develop employees, as well as attract potential workers.

Figure 4.10 below shows a small fraction of the linkages between people value and other key business elements. Consider the impact of capacity and capacity utilization on employee, customer and shareholder value. A company without sufficient capacity to serve its customers will cause service delays, diminishing customer-perceived quality. Insufficient capacity will place stress on employees because, like NationJet's check-in staff, they are probably working as fast as they can to serve waiting customers, and customers who have to wait will be less pleasant to deal with. This situation can be self-correcting as discouraged customers defect to competitors. These defections would reduce revenue and probably shareholder value as well. If customers do not defect at a rate sufficient to bring capacity in line with demand, then employees will begin to burn out. The remaining employees will be forced to bear even larger workloads as their burned out colleagues quit or take disability leave. Diminished capacity will result in greater service delays and potentially a death spiral for the business.

Figure 4.10   Modeling Employee Value

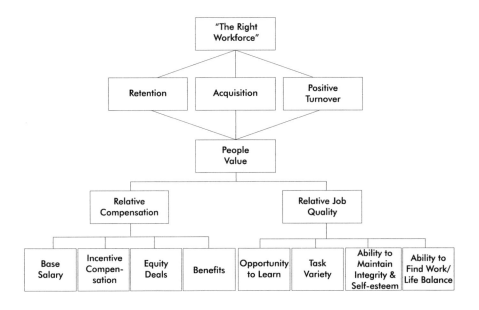

Employee value is a function of both job quality and compensation relative to what the employee could realize at a different job. Attributes of job quality can be determined through employee focus groups and measured from time to time through the use of employee value surveys. Relative compensation is a function of several attributes such as base salary, incentive compensation, equity arrangements and benefits. Relative job quality is also a function of several attributes and subattributes. There are numerous examples of job-quality attributes and subattributes that address issues such as commitment, employee satisfaction and capability, as shown in Figure 4.11.

Relative perceived job quality and compensation combine to yield the employee value of the job. This, relative to jobs available from other employers, determines the company's ability to retain employees and attract new ones. It is worth observing that different employees value different attributes of perceived job quality. For instance, job-related travel is viewed positively by some people and negatively by others. The nature of the business and company policy will determine a company's attributes of job quality. The attributes profile will attract some people and discourage others.

Figure 4.11 People Performance Measures/Attribute Tree

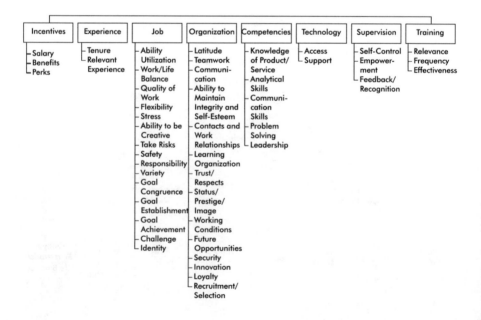

Moreover, some people will make greater productive contributions to an enterprise than others. If a company's attributes of job quality fail to retain employees who are making greater productive contributions to an enterprise, this is called "negative turnover." On the other hand, if a company's attributes of job quality fail to retain employees who are not making productive contributions to an enterprise, then we call this "positive turnover."

Managing people value requires careful integration into the management process through a method of defining attributes and measures of people value, relating people measures to shareholder value measures, relating people measures to customer measures and implementing programs to enhance people value attributes. This approach is shown on the next page in Figure 4.12.

NationJet was able to implement an enterprise value scorecard (Figure 4.13) by looking at a cash flow view of the business instead of the traditional earnings perspective, developing a customer value perspective of the business that will replace the traditional customer satisfaction survey reports, and establish a people value scorecard. The company was still in for some surprises, including discovering that it actually had negative cash flow despite positive earnings, a stunning discovery on its customer value map, and an unexpected insight in employee value.

This was only the beginning for NationJet and any other company that undertakes the Value Journey. While it is important to measure and understand the enterprise value that a company has and is creating, it is also important to gain some sense for the value the company is likely to create in the future. In fact, that value is what is most relevant to the stakeholders. Customers will prefer to buy from others and avoid switching costs if they perceive that the company will not offer the most attractive value proposition in the future. Employees will look elsewhere if they don't foresee value in remaining with the company. Shareholders value a company largely on the future cash flows it is expected to generate. But how do we develop an understanding of the enterprise value that a company will probably generate in the future? The answer is found in value modeling, which is discussed in the next chapter.

Figure 4.12 People Value Management — Model

A three-stage framework for developing People Value Management capabilities.

Stage 2
Relate People Value Measures to Shareholder Value Measures and Customer Value Measures

Stage 1
Determine measures of People Value and Key Attributes that drive value

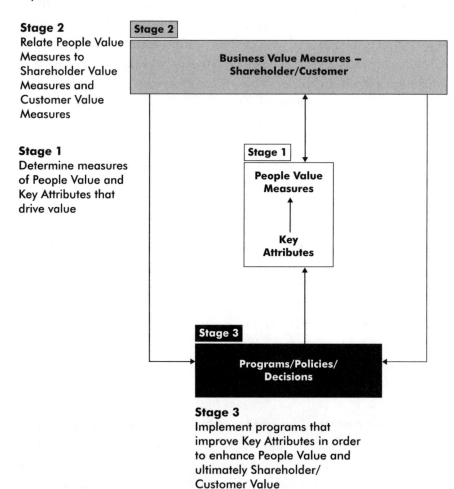

Stage 3
Implement programs that improve Key Attributes in order to enhance People Value and ultimately Shareholder/Customer Value

Figure 4.13   NationJet's Enterprise Value Scorecard

Cash Flow (in $ M)	Actual	Target	Previous	Explanation	Actions
Revenue	2,500	2,550	2,450	Retention rate falling for non-business	Improve service levels in non-business
Expense	2,100	2,120	2,070	Staffing levels assumed higher non-business volume	
Cash from Operations	400	430	380		
Cash investments	250	230	240	Advanced ticket sales decline	
Cash flow before Financing	150	200	140		

Customer Value (Passenger segment)					
Relative price	105%	105%	110%	Matched competitor discounts	
Routing	8.2	8.1	8.0		
On-time performance	7.9	8.2	8.1	On-time performance declined 10%	Alleviate scheduling pressure
Comfort	8.5	8.5	8.6		
Friendliness/PVA	8.7	9.0	8.9	Time pressure hurt morale	Alleviate time pressure
Safety	9.2	9.0	9.0		
Relative quality	8.3	8.5	8.4		
Relative value	8.1	8.3	8.2		
Churn	13%	8%	10%		
Change in market share	-.3%	.1%	-.1%		
Change in life time value	-$260	$100	-$110		

Employee Value					
Relative compensation	105%	105%	105%		
Culture	7.7	8.1	7.8	Time pressure has hurt morale	Alleviate time pressure
Challenge	7.8	8.1	7.8		
Learning	7.9	8.2	7.7		
Relative quality	7.8	8.1	7.8		
Relative value	8.2	8.5	8.2		
Positive turnover	1%	3%	1%		
Negative turnover	4%	2%	5%		
New hires	90	80	125		

Chapter 5

VALUE MODELING
Putting the Elements Together

NationJet's CEO, George Braga, had a few hectic months getting his airline to support the concept of managing for enterprise value. While staff had eagerly adopted the concepts of thinking about value from the perspective of shareholder, customer and employee, it was not a simple process. At the senior levels, developing the Enterprise Value Scorecard was relatively straightforward. Pushing the measures down to the operational level, however, created many challenges. Many operations managers had never had performance measures or had the same performance measures for the past ten years. They had been achieving their performance targets over the course of that time and wondered why they should switch now. The exercise of educating managers of the need to change consumed a significant amount of Braga's time.

There were successes though. Some staff members enthusiastically embraced the opportunity to focus their work on real outcomes. For example, several members of the marketing group worked with the scheduling team to make minor schedule changes and develop new fare options for flights that were traditionally only three-quarters full. They clearly demonstrated that value would be produced for a modest investment.

For the first time, the organization had a clear and comprehensive scorecard that supported the company's mission and helped quantify whether it was creating value. Now that NationJet knew what to focus on, a new problem emerged. The employees had begun identifying key opportunities and business changes that they believed would help them achieve the value creating outcomes. Unfortunately, some of the suggestions were seriously at odds with the others.

For example, one of the marketing staff suggested a multiple-bookings option for frequent business travelers, many of whom were already making repeat bookings to ensure they could get on a flight. This option would build loyalty as people with uncertain schedules could be assured of getting a seat, with a minor cost of implementing the changes in the reservation system. This idea contradicted one of the reservations managers' suggestions for improving scheduling and generating some revenue by charging people who double book the cost of their seat because they overload the reservation system and result in planes that are not completely full. She reasoned that the resulting reduction in plane occupancy reduced revenue and actually inconvenienced more people than the charge for double booking would hurt customer loyalty.

Braga suddenly recognized that he was concentrating too much on value outcomes, and that NationJet did not have a common view about where and how value was created in the organization. While most of the employees wanted to solve known problems and exploit key opportunities, many lacked the capacity to understand the cross-impacts that their suggestions would have on other functional areas. Braga realized that he had merely scratched the surface of the organizational change required to become a value enterprise.

Like NationJet, any company faces a steep challenge in coming to terms with enterprise value. Most managers are frustrated continually when they attempt to predict their decisions' potential impacts. While they are usually able to assess short-term financial impacts on costs or revenues, an integrated assessment of the trade-offs for long-term cash flows, revenues, costs and capital proves elusive. Often, they end up with conflicting ad hoc analyses and waste much time arguing. And this is often the easy part. When it comes to a thoughtful analysis of the effect operational changes have on customer service or employee satisfaction, most companies have no conceptual model to assess trade-offs.

The functional silos created, and the time lag between cause and effect in this business were unlike anything George Braga had ever seen. He sought the counsel of trusted friends. One, a key executive at a major aircraft manufacturer, is frequently cited in trade publications and by corporate awards for stellar performance. Braga's friend told him about value modeling and its significant success in managing the very issues that NationJet was then addressing. Braga began to explore what value modeling is and what it could do for his company. It quickly became evident that value modeling was essential if Braga was to change his company's culture permanently and establish a value enterprise.

What exactly is a value model? It is a facsimile of a company's business reality. Models can be physical, such as a child's plastic models of cars and aircraft: you can't travel in them but they often show a remarkable likeness to the real thing. Or think of those small-scale pilot plants that engineers build to prove the technical and economic viability of a full-scale production system. They physically demonstrate everything a big factory would do without the financial commitment of building the real thing. Value models are not physical, but rather conceptual and mathematical facsimiles that show how a business works to generate enterprise value.

Braga's friend likened the value model to a flight simulator, a pseudo-cockpit on hydraulic legs that mimics an airliner's behavior in astonishing detail. With the flight simulator, the airline can expose its pilots to every scenario a big aircraft could encounter, both likely and unlikely, without the expense and danger of the real thing. So it is with a value model. Instead of using sophisticated computer graphics to create busy airports and changing weather conditions outside the flight simulator's windshield, the value model can simulate a wide variety of situations that the corporate machine can encounter. By changing the inputs, the value-model operator can provide dramatically detailed alternatives to real business situations.

The value model enables management to tweak and pull at operations to see how, under different conditions, the company would perform, just as pilots test their skills in a flight simulator against a range of possible events. What happens at NationJet if it adds capacity with another plane? What impact will that decision have on tangibles such as fleet usage and load factors and even on intangibles such as customer satisfaction? If the airplane is a small, fuel-efficient Canadair Regional Jet it will enable the airline to serve thinly traveled routes that it could not accommodate with larger craft. But passengers may not feel as comfortable in its small 50-seat cabin. The value models allow testing of these types of scenarios to assess their impacts without trying them in real life.

Thanks to recent advances in computing and software, value models can accommodate and integrate a wide variety of financial and non-financial information with scenario and risk analysis, random number and random distribution generators, and optimization modules, all standard on most spreadsheet programs. With these tools, managers can model far more elaborately than ever before, looking at a range of outcomes instead of the dangerously misleading game of averages.

In his book, *Industrial Dynamics*, Jay Forrester sums up modeling:

> [With a model,] circumstances can be studied that might seldom be encountered in the real world. Daring changes that might seem too risky to try with an actual company can be investigated. [With modeling,] the manager ... can now have a laboratory in which he can learn quickly and at low cost the answers that would seldom be obtainable from trials on real organizations.[1]

But value modeling isn't only about testing new scenarios. It is about viewing a company holistically as a system and understanding the behaviors and events caused by underlying structures and interrelationships within the system. As Peter Senge describes in *The Fifth Discipline*:

> Modeling is a shift of mind from seeing parts to seeing wholes, from seeing managers as helpless reactors to seeing them as active participants in shaping their reality, from reacting to the present to creating the future.[2]

The purpose of value modeling is to create understanding and communication of how a business works to produce the enterprise value. Value creation will be a function of the variety of factors that will interact to affect enterprise value both inside and outside the company. Figure 5.1 illustrates how a model crosses the boundaries of the three forms of value and captures the inter- and intradivisional relationships, leading to value creation.

A value perspective comes through understanding and communicating the value perspective at every level. Those fundamentals must become the nuts and bolts of a manager's domain. As Forrester states:

Figure 5.1   Enterprise Value Model Linkages

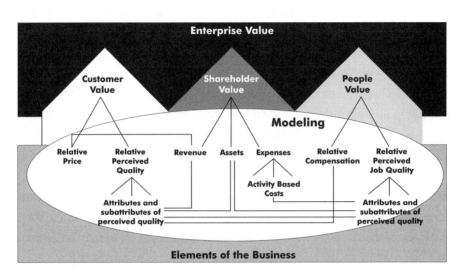

A model can point the way to policies that yield more favorable performance [...] It should show how changes in company structure or policy will produce better or worse behavior. It should show the kinds of external disturbance to which the system is vulnerable.[3]

Braga knew that he had to revise the company's management framework to see where it was really heading. He started by asking where value creation actually takes place. The value factors of any business are not determined at the senior executive level or in the financial department. They reside deep in the operations process, at the grassroots level. Value is created in operations – in the maintenance base, on the tarmac, at the check-in counter, on the flight deck. The key data he was looking for were not *financial* but *operational*. Properly analyzed and understood, operations data can forecast actual financial performance. But more importantly, management can understand how to use operating parameters to maximize value created under various circumstances. With a model, the company can arrive at an operational view of its business that converts a standard financial statement into operating parameters where the outcomes are financial. This provides managers with relevant and applicable value-creating information, as opposed to those pages of traditional financial data they are accustomed to and somewhat estranged from.

Most companies already have financial models as well as operational systems that capture much of the data they need to make key decisions. The operational view of business a value model generates is the merger of these two disciplines. It provides a helpful understanding of how day-to-day activities affect enterprise value.

Value modeling provides a company with tools to understand future value by pulling all relevant corporate and market information together, integrating it in a holistic fashion. It also allows a company to understand the important interrelationships between its business units and functional areas. Building value models would help NationJet to sort out how its operations and marketing divisions affect one another and how both *jointly* affect the corporation's creation of value. The resulting models can identify where there are intracompany "disconnects," gaps in communications where the essence and understanding of value creation remains in the hands of a few senior executives. These insiders do not communicate their knowledge to the rest of the company who must create that value, so value creation strategy gets stunted. Moreover, modeling helps pinpoint customer and employee attributes of value, something that can seem ethereal and elusive in the physical world of business. Value-based management calls for a comprehensive, dynamic view of a business so a company can identify any unintended intracompany conflicts and understand the trade-offs needed to balance departments.

NationJet's managers need a common view of the world so they can make informed assumptions on where to focus their efforts and, just as important, where not to waste their time. Value modeling provides this insight through a common understanding of how the company's customers, assets, activities and employees interrelate to affect future cash flows. How the parts relate can affect those flows and the analysis of its expected future cash flows. By understanding holistically where their cash flows come from, NationJet executives will be able to target where and how they should concentrate on value creation.

So far, NationJet had left far too much to random decisions. There were unexpected and unwelcome side effects to their efforts, which sometimes chain-reacted to destroy value in an insidious way. Take cost cutting. Operations had slashed labor costs through layoffs at the check-in counter. In the short term, the remaining staff picked up the slack and overall perfor-mance remained stable with fewer staff. Managers began to believe that they must have been overstaffed before the layoffs, so they congratulated them-selves on correct instincts. But then, the surviving staff began to burn out and their performance dropped precipitously. Customers faced longer lines and they were not happy about it. Business travelers were glancing over at Budget Airways' nearby counters. They had short, fast-moving lines, so why were NationJet's business passengers paying higher fares to stand in line?

Then there was NationJet's aggressive policy of overbooking. Passengers stood a real chance of getting bumped off flights after having endured the long check-in wait. The plane would probably be late anyhow, since NationJet kept its planes flying so long there was little turnaround time left for ground crews on the ramp. They were tripping over themselves to keep to the tight schedule, growing more alienated with their work by the day. Baggage han-dlers' injuries were way up and so were lost bags. Of course, the check-in staff did not know that the ramp crews were overworked, behind in their work, and thus delaying flights. Given half the chance they would grumble to customers that nobody in management tells check-in staff anything. That was because operations managers probably did not know why it was happening.

Managers do not understand that when they lay off staff they are only considering the cost side of their operations, not the benefit side. Value mod-eling will help Braga build a value "case" for NationJet, and implement a company-wide understanding of the relationships and trade-offs between divi-sions and functions. His model will integrate all aspects of the company and focus on how the company's activities will affect future cash flow at all levels.

Braga's management team had little idea what a value model was, and that was not surprising, since value modeling is relatively new. As recently as ten years ago, modeling was an enormous analytical undertaking, such that it was the preserve of small groups of scientists and operations researchers located in some remote part of a company with huge backlogs of statistics and analysis. They focused on one problem at a time and took months to analyze it. As a result, decisions about change came slowly and the results were confined to those back rooms and perhaps the boardroom, but rarely shared with operations. Most companies have more information than they know what to do with. They have vast amounts of data they cannot interpret and apply to appropriate operating units. Only in recent years, thanks to computers, spreadsheet analysis software and numerous enhancements have the tools for value modeling come to managers' desks.

Through the process of gathering the information needed to formulate a model, it can be quite instructive to discover how a company's employees and management learn. The way people retain and disseminate information helps to understand how and why a company should be modeled. The owner of a corner milk store has no concerns about how his or her actions will affect employees in other divisions because he or she has no other employees. But in a multilayered company, it becomes a real problem getting managers to understand the consequences of their actions across the company. Modeling is all about discovering where trade-offs must be made for the good of the company and then making the situation relevant to mangers and, finally, creating checks and balances to handle trade-offs. Senge describes this process:

> Traditionally, organizations attempt to surmount the difficulty of coping
> with the breadth of impact from decision by breaking themselves up
> into components that are easier for people to get their hands around.
> But, functional divisions grow into fiefdoms, and what was once a con-
> venient division of labour mutates into the "stove pipes" that all but cut
> off contact between functions. The result: analysis of the most impor-
> tant problems in a company, the complex issues that cross functional
> lines, becomes a perilous or non-existent exercise.[4]

Business-units become good at mastering what goes on in their domain or the functional hierarchy. But knowledge of how their actions affect other areas of the company is often completely unknown. Such is the case with NationJet, where vice presidents for operations and sales and marketing peer across the hall at one another, each only vaguely understanding what his counterpart does and not seeing how their joint activities direct – or misdirect – the airline. This is all too common: the silo effect that Senge described as "stove pipes," or the intracompany disconnect we identified earlier.

There is another problem: the way humans gather and synthesize infor-
mation. NationJet managers were firm believers in creating value by actively managing their head-count numbers and keeping them as low as possible. They rationalized this with what they felt was the high cost of their unionized workforce, and partly the fact that "they'd always done things that way."

In fact, in all companies there is a fact-gathering hierarchy that presides over much of the information, generalizations and even myths of how the company operates. We call it the learning pyramid (see Figure 5.2). At the bottom are the volumes of raw data fed to the system by employees throughout the organization. As the information is sent up the organization, however, there is a tendency for information handlers to filter it, groom it, compartmentalize it and offer prescriptions for it. It is an easy trap for busy senior executives to fall into, relying on prepared information with accompanying

Figure 5.2   The Learning Pyramid

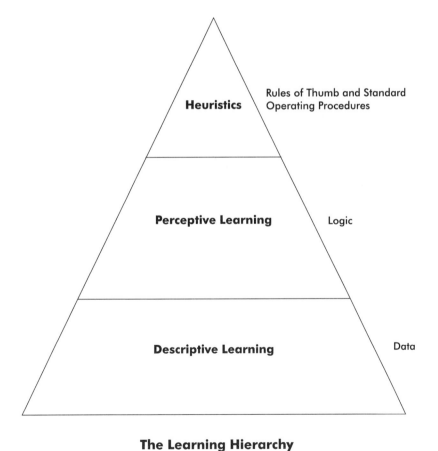

Heuristics — Rules of Thumb and Standard Operating Procedures

Perceptive Learning — Logic

Descriptive Learning — Data

The Learning Hierarchy

prescriptions. Sometimes those prescriptions are only dangerously inaccurate approximations of what needs to be done.

Yet companies cling to this way of doing business without any mechanism for assessing its effectiveness. This is how misinformation becomes the foundation for business assumptions. At the top of the pyramid are the heuristics, the rules of thumb that eventually become the company's frame of reference. Employees often explain why they do their jobs in a certain way, despite the fact that it may be irrelevant to creating value for the company, just like NationJet. It is not hard to see how heuristics get passed from generation to generation. Through this process these heuristics become the standard operating procedures and become entrenched in the organization. When the organization experiences a change in the environment, such as deregulation, the inertia from these operating procedures may slow the company's response to the new environment.

When these heuristics are identified and challenged, however, it does not take a lot of modeling to realize the correct rules of thumb may have changed. For NationJet, management discovered that staff cutbacks were resulting in significant direct costs of increased overtime as well as other detrimental effects, such as decreased morale and poorer customer service, along with an increased number of on-the-job accidents and the ensuing insurance claims.

One of the important reasons for modeling is to make the perceptions management has of its organization explicit and fact-based, and then share the information systematically with employees. Senge sums up the merits of managing mental models:

> Nothing undermines openness more surely than certainty. Once we feel we have the answer, all motivation to question our thinking disappears . . . New insights fail to get put into practice because they conflict with a deeply held internal image of how the world works.[5]

> That is why the discipline of managing mental models – surfacing, testing, and improving our internal pictures of how the world works – promises to be a major breakthrough for building effective learning organizations.[6]

A second important reason for constructing models is that managers stay a relatively short time in their positions, typically three years or less. As a result, decision making and subsequent work procedures becomes an inheritance from previous holders of that position. Scores of value-creating opportunities get lost as new managers come up to speed in their new positions. Value is fleeting: precision and speed are prerequisites for capturing it, and that requires accurate information. Capturing the learnings of the organization can become an important part of sustaining value creation through a transition in management of a function.

When a company commits to value-based management, it finds it has to rebuild its heuristics and recognize the need to revisit them continuously as the business climate changes. When George Braga began to stack together a model of his information hierarchy, the intricacies of the dynamics emerged. He began to clarify how a series of perceptions might have been slightly or even massively erroneous. Value modeling uncovers these phenomena. It can create a reliable facsimile for each area of the business, which then sets the stage for much faster, ongoing learning about how each area of the business can create value creation for the entire enterprise.

How to Build a Model

It is essential to understand the business' constituent parts and how they work together and will work together to produce enterprise value now and in the future. The key steps to developing this understanding are:

- defining the model's scope
- determining a modeling technique
- identifying the model elements
- linking them
- calibrating the model
- putting the model into operation

DEFINING MODEL SCOPE

It is important to realize that there will not be one single business model which will address all the issues and concerns regarding the different forms of value creation. Managers will use different models depending upon their focus and the level of detail required for the decision at hand. Some models may tackle specific issues directed at a specific stakeholder; others may take an enterprise view, integrating parts from all three forms of value creation. What all models have in common is that value is the language of their outputs.

In defining the model scope, the type of value model to be built must be chosen. The choices will be driven by the kind of issues that need to be addressed on the following dimensions:

- Breadth of organizational focus (enterprise-wide vs. business issue vs. business process vs. business unit models); and

- Depth of detail complexity (modeling customers or products in aggregate or individually).

Broad, enterprise-wide value models can help to understand, at a high level, how all of the pieces of the business work together to create enterprise value. The enterprise-wide value model helps identify the high-level value drivers throughout the business. At the other end of spectrum are business unit, business process or issue-specific value models. These more focused models do not incorporate all parts of the enterprise. Instead, they drill deeper into the activities, attributes and relationships that are relevant to the issue or business unit being examined. The focused models are used to more comprehensively identify the value drivers for the business unit, process or issue at lower levels in the organization. Issue-specific models can be very narrow in scope and, therefore, quicker to design and build. Enterprise-wide, business unit or business process value models, that are likely to be used for multiple issues, inquiries and decisions need to be more flexible, making them more difficult to design and build.

Creating a model that is both broad and deep is nearly impossible. Models become more complex as more elements and relationships are added. Models that are both broad and deep tend to be complex and difficult to understand. Replicating reality with a complex model that reveals few insights about what drives value in the business defeats the purpose of value modeling. Remember, the purpose of modeling is to create and communicate understanding. To do this, a balance needs to be struck between excessive complexity, which doesn't lead to understanding, and simplicity, which doesn't create any insights.

DETERMINING MODELING TECHNIQUE

Once the scope of the model has been determined, the most appropriate technique must be selected. The technique chosen will depend on additional factors such as the data available, the completion deadline, the desired detail and accuracy level and the level of effort and resources that can be committed to modeling. Models can be divided into two groups, either static or dynamic. Static models do not have feedback mechanisms built in, whereas dynamic models capture the time-delayed impacts of feedback. Dynamic models come in two forms: continuous models and discrete models.

Static value models are most commonly implemented in spreadsheets. What makes them static is that they have fixed time frames and do not use feedback within the model. Despite their similarity to most spreadsheet models, these should not be confused with the financial models found on most managers' computers. In the NationJet finance department, the managers there thought they already had a value model, as do their counterparts in many companies. But too often what they have are elaborate spreadsheets which are only navigable by those who created them. In other cases, they have used financial planning tools but only to create accounting-based cost budgets. In others, there are rudimentary linkages to operational drivers, especially in industries that have few drivers. For example, in the gas business, price is a key input and drives most of the value. Real value models are few in number. Most companies have financial planning models but few have linked their operational drivers and very few use the models as management and operational decision making tools. As John Sterman points out in *The Fifth Discipline Fieldbook:*

> No one denies that spreadsheets are useful. But they also lowered the technical barriers facing people who wanted to do financial modeling. As a result, in the first few years after the introduction of spreadsheets, the average quality of financial models plummeted. Today, many financial models are not only useless, but downright harmful to decision makers who build them.[7]

There are several differences between ordinary financial models and value models:

- Value models have better defined linkages between financial results and operational drivers, putting the focus on operations, not finance.

- Customer value, employee value and cash flow is the common language in value models, while financial models may measure performance through different techniques or not focus on value at all.

- Value models are used throughout the organization, putting them in the hands of operations managers with an easy to use graphical user interface, whereas many financial models are frequently only understood by their authors

- Value models have several modules that allow users to understand their business better and to make value-creating decisions making the tool a living decision-support tool not a one time financial snapshot.

- Value models incorporate the dynamics of business-linking decisions and costs to the benefit using the appropriate value measurements. Financial models traditionally allow users to enter revenue and cost projections independently by year with few real-life checks and balances. The financial model serves as nothing more than a calculator.

With dynamic modeling, the objective is to model the operation of a business system. Remember that the definition of a system is a collection of elements that interact with each other to function as a whole. The goal is to model the causal relationships and the associated lag times between elements of the system and assess the impact on the three forms of value creation.

Dynamic models differ from static ones in that they operate in continuous time rather than the fixed time increments imposed by the rows and columns in a spreadsheet. In addition, dynamic models typically (but not necessarily) incorporate the time delayed feedback found within most systems. While most managers understand the concepts of dynamic systems at a conceptual level, until recently, putting them into practice had proven difficult due to the sophisticated computational mathematics involved. The decrease in the cost of computer processing power has allowed for the development of sophisticated system dynamics modeling tools with user-friendly interfaces which can be used to understand how the feedback structure of business systems generate observed patterns of behavior.

Creating dynamic models requires a shift in thinking about what happens within a business system. In a static world, one focuses on events, and understanding the details. In a dynamic world one thinks about behavior over time and understanding relationships and the structures that drive the behaviors.

For example, referring back to Figure 5.1, in a static model the objective is to understand, for example, how changing employee activities can impact customer value. In a dynamic system, how the customer's reaction to those changing activities may in turn impact the future demand for those original activities must also be considered. In creating dynamic models the techniques most commonly used are either continuous systems modeling or discrete event modeling.

For continuous systems modeling, a modeling technique pioneered in the 1960s by Jay Forrester called the "Systems Dynamics" method is used. Systems Dynamics is an approach to modeling that addresses how the feedback structure of complex systems generates observed patterns of behavior. The nature of continuous models forces us to think at a higher level about the elements within the model. Instead of thinking about customers as individuals with specific behavior, think of them in general terms and look for opportunities to segment and group them based on their behaviors. In other words, deal with the forest as a whole, not tree by tree.

To model to a more detailed level and capture the behavior of individual items (customers, employees, assets) discrete event modeling needs to be used. Items within the model retain individual identities and can be assigned specific actions and behaviors based on operating conditions at that exact point in time. Using this technique, sophisticated business process models can be created and the value-creating impacts of operational decisions observed. This technique is ideal for modeling physical processes (such as customers arriving and queuing in a bank, or parts being assembled on an assembly line), but it does depend on detailed process and activity data.

IDENTIFYING MODEL ELEMENTS

The purpose of identifying model elements is to create an inventory of all the significant parts the model should have. Model elements are the operational parameters that will be linked into the enterprise value measurement. For example, looking at the revenue side of the shareholder value equation, typically the first step is to break Revenue down into Quantity times Price. Quantity could be further broken down by market region or perhaps into Total Market Demand times Market Share. Similarly, price can be modeled using customer value analysis as it has been described in Chapter 4. The goal is to break down the business enough to get value insights without introducing too much complexity in terms of modeling the business or in understanding the model once it is complete.

An enterprise-wide model does not need a lot of operational detail and probably won't need to reflect every other part of the business in a more focused model. Similarly, in a more focused model, there isn't a need to reflect every other part of the business. With an understanding of the areas to be modeled and the level at which they will be modeled, these areas are then decomposed into their constituent parts. How is it possible to know which parts are significant? It might be possible to guess at some of them, but one of the most important objectives of value modeling is to identify elements that, thus far, have not been recognized as significant. This is why modeling is a continuous, iterative learning process. Only when the model of the elements is constructed and tested, can the value significance of each element be understood. It's the chicken before the egg dilemma. What should come first – identifying model elements or building the model? The most elegant models begin with the identification of model elements.

When identifying model elements, however, do not try to be too exhaustive in the first round. Start by identifying model elements. Then construct a model and test it. Finally, assess whether the model sufficiently reflects the behavior of the business. If it does not, there are probably additional elements that need to be identified and incorporated into the model. In most instances, two to three iterations of model development will produce a reasonable model. This can take anywhere from one to six months. After that, a company will probably go through another process of model development every six months to two years. Will the model ever be completed? Probably not, unless the model is perfect and the enterprise's environment will never change, or the organization stops learning. The first situation is not likely and hopefully the second situation is just as unlikely.

Here are some useful sources for identifying the model elements. Attributes of customer and employee value are available from the customer and people value models described in Chapter Four. A business's physical assets are usually recorded in its accounting books. Planned acquisition of physical assets is typically documented in capital spending plans. Maps and information of the company's processes are likely to exist if the company has done or attempted reengineering (most have). An activity-based costing system will provide an inventory of the company's activities and their cost behavior. Data illustrating the behavior of model elements over time is extremely valuable in assessing causal relationships for use in dynamic models.

This information provides a rich start to value modeling. Don't fret if you don't have all this data. Few companies do. For many organizations, one of the chief benefits of the value modeling exercise is the identification of information that they don't have, but really need to manage effectively. At this point many clients take initiatives to fill these gaps. Does this mean value modeling must stop until the gaps are filled? No. Don't sit and wait for the data gaps to be filled before starting the modeling process. Many companies have filled information gaps by relying on managers' best guesses. After all, that's what they've been using to run the company to this point. Later, when the information becomes available, they will replace or validate the guesses.

How are model elements flushed out where the information is lacking? One tool that has proved useful is the value tree. Value trees are not only useful in helping decompose a business into its constituent elements, they also help point out some of the relationships between elements. The most common approach to building a value tree is to start with cash flow at the top and then to break down the elements that result in cash flow. Approaches that start with cash flow are probably most common because companies are much more fluent in, and familiar with, financial terms and perspectives. Most companies already have financial models for their business that will resemble the value tree.

Value decomposition starts with identifying a value-focused goal. Then, operating components are linked to the different constituents of that goal. For example, let's consider NationJet's operating expenses. As illustrated in

Figure 5.3 the major operating expenses in an airline are salaries, fuel, meals and entertainment, maintenance, general and administration and airport fees. Note that these items may be on the financial statements as subcomponents of operating expenses. Take maintenance and decompose it further. From an activity point of view, two types of maintenance are performed: turnaround (between flights) and operating (scheduled maintenance). The drivers for the activities are the number of flights (for turnaround maintenance) and the number of planes (for scheduled maintenance).

Materials and staff are required, depending on the level of activity defined by the drivers. For those acquainted with activity-based costing (ABC), this process of decomposition as shown in Figure 5.4 may seem familiar. The activity view that is taken in value decomposition often means a linkage with ABC, and is often leveraged strongly off ABC work that has already been done. In this way, the utility of ABC work and the value models that are created using the ABC relationships increases.

Figure 5.3   Operating Expenses Decomposition

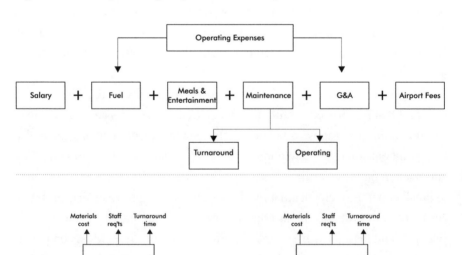

Figure 5.4   Value Decomposition

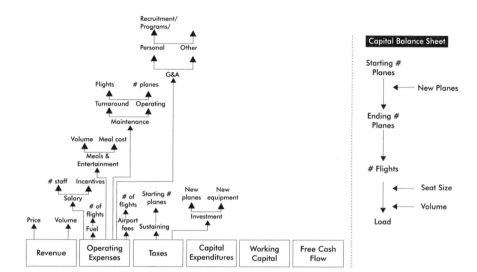

LINKING MODEL ELEMENTS

Once most of the significant elements of the business have been identified, it is time to start modeling. Modeling is almost the reverse of decomposition. One might ask, why bother decomposing reality into elements only to recompose the elements into a model? The reason to go through this exercise is to produce a version of reality that is free of a lot of detail. The simplified version of reality provides a much clearer view of how the most fundamental parts of the business work. As John Holland points out in *Hidden Order*:

> Modeling, it should be clear, is an art form. It depends on the experience and taste of the modeler. In this it is much like cartooning, especially political cartooning. The modeler (cartoonist) must decide which features to make salient (exaggerate), and which features to eliminate (avoid), in order to answer the questions (make the political point).[8]

Value trees are a good place to start with value modeling. Begin modeling by connecting elements between various branches of the value trees. Figure 5.5 provides an example of these connections.

Figure 5.5   Value Map

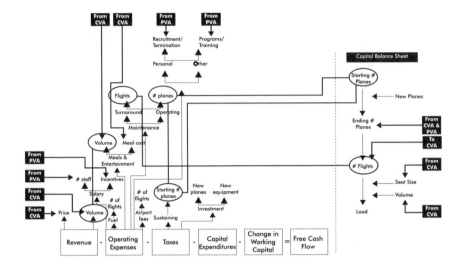

*   CVA – Customer Value Attributes
    PVA – People Value Attributes

Notice how the value trees lose their simple hierarchical structure. The result is typically something that looks like a network diagram, and is usually referred to as a value map. A value map is a powerful tool. It helps show how all of the company's processes, activities, assets and constituents (customers and employees) work together. This perspective is especially beneficial for executives, managers and employees who have a limited view of how their particular function or process relates to others in the business. A value map can allow the production group to see how R&D ultimately impacts production costs, and how production costs affect sales. Figure 5.6 is a value map from E.I du Pont de Nemours and Co.

By forcing the clarification and quantification of the assumptions and intuitive rules of thumb used by operating managers, inconsistencies and contradictions that must be addressed can be discovered. Note that quantifiable and measurable are not synonymous. In fact, intuitively we know that this is not the case. While the motivation of the baggage handlers at NationJet

Figure 5.6   DuPont Value Map

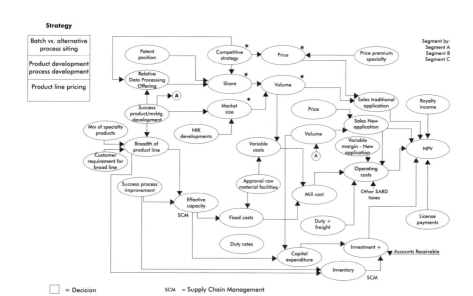

Source: *Cash Flow and Performance Measurement*:
Managing for Value by Henry A. Davis, 1996

cannot be precisely measured, it can certainly be quantified on a scale of 1 to 20. From that we can begin to understand some of the factors that might drive motivation (e.g., satisfaction, compensation, working conditions), and what might be the resultant impacts of higher or lower motivation.

It is also important to remember when establishing relationships within the model, that correlation does not imply causality. The fact that two variables appear to move in tandem, does not mean that one *causes* the other. For example, when the tulips begin to bloom we also observe that people begin to wear lighter clothing outside. These events are perfectly correlated, but one did not cause the other.

CALIBRATING THE MODEL

The working model must be tested against real data from the company to determine if it is producing results known to be false. If it does, then the model must be adjusted before proceeding. The assumptions and linkage must be revisited with an eye on reproducing a reference behavior. Calibration involves creating a hypothesis and testing if the model can support the hypothesis. If the model does not, then there can be two areas of concern. The first is that the model isn't correct, and the second, often overlooked, factor is that the data testing the model may not be correct. To address the former, revisit the assumptions and linkages. To address the data, recognize that just because data exists in a system, it may not be correct, due to errors in measurement, collection or filtering, or it may not be the right data for the model.

The key question to ask is not: "Is the model a perfect representation of reality," because it never will be. Rather, the question should be: "Based on my expertise in this business do the results make sense?" If they don't, then revisit the model. Similarly the model must be stretched to understand what are the ranges of operating parameters over which it behaves in a certain manner. What if passenger demand is increased by 400%. What if the operating staff is cut in half? What if the fleet is reduced by 75%. While these are not likely scenarios for NationJet (or so George Braga hopes in some cases), the ways our models respond to them tell us a great deal. This is where you learn what are the sensitive points – the value drivers that are worthy of more attention.

PUTTING THE MODEL INTO OPERATION

Once a model is created, it needs to be put to work. That means subjecting it to sensitivity and scenario analysis, testing policies and continuously modifying it and improving it. It cannot be overly emphasized that the process of creating models is one of learning and communication. Essential parts of this communication activity are the documentation of the model, and training users in its effective and appropriate use. This does not mean having users read documentation and play with the model for half an hour; it entails workshops in which people interact to share their views on how the business functions. The most powerful learning occurs when managers from different functions are brought together to work with a model. In the ensuing discussions of the assumptions, it is not uncommon that managers from one area have diametrically opposing assumptions to their counterparts in other functions. The process of using the model brings those contradictions to the surface, educates the managers and makes the model that much more accurate. In some cases, the model becomes secondary to the conversations and collective understanding of managers — the model becomes a learning tool to facilitate their discussions.

The deployment of the infrastructure to support these models involves the people using the models, the technology infrastructure supporting them, and the process of maintaining them. These will be dealt with extensively in Chapter Nine.

In using the models, it is important that they are approached correctly. Rather than "black boxes" which magically provides answers, models must be viewed as tools to facilitate the understanding of how the enterprise creates value. This will include sensitivity and scenario testing, as well as the evaluation of new policies and strategies. Once again, if the model is inconsistent with the real world, then this is an opportunity to push further in the iterative development process and expand your organizational learning capability.

While the models show the outcomes of scenarios, they cannot predict the likelihood of those scenarios occurring. For example, NationJet could have scenarios for dealing with future economic growth (a recession, flat economy or economic boom) and their associated impacts on NationJet's market, with some alternative responses to those scenarios. The wrong action is to predict, or as some companies do, have one or several people *vote* on the expected future scenario that is most likely, and act accordingly. As will be seen in Chapter 8, the right thing to do is to understand what the models are telling us and the implications of choosing a certain path and plan appropriately.

NationJet — A Sample High-Level Model

NationJet's CEO decided that his organization would start by building an enterprise-wide model of its business. He wanted to develop a high-level understanding of how all of the major parts of the business work together to create value and share this understanding throughout the organization. Braga also wanted to discover and confirm NationJet's high-level value drivers, so that he and his team could focus on and manage these drivers. Several of NationJet's vice presidents were interested in developing value models that were specific to their part of the business. They wanted to gain a deeper understanding of the value drivers within their business units. The business-unit value models will be started once the company made significant progress in developing the high-level enterprise-wide model for NationJet.

Based on the high-level scope George Braga defined and the availability of existing financial and activity based costing data, it was determined that a static value model was the best route to follow. The NationJet modeling team began with a high-level view of what they wanted to capture in the model as shown in Figure 5.7. The question then was which part to start with. The readily available financial data gave them an opportunity to start on the shareholder value analysis section while the data was gathered for the other parts of the model.

Figure 5.7   Value Model Conceptual Design

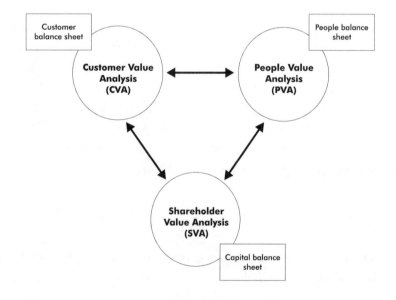

From the initial financial data they received, the team transformed the pro forma income statements and balance sheets into cash flows. Then they discounted the pro forma cash flows and terminal valuation of cash flows expected beyond the pro forma horizon to arrive at the warranted value of the business as shown in Figure 5.8.

Figure 5.8   Financial Model Yielding Cash Flows and Warranted Value

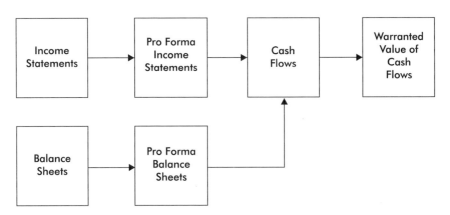

To complete the first iteration of the value model the NationJet team replaced the actual (or historic) income statement and balance sheet with a model of the company's operations which populates the pro forma income statement and balance sheet. Figure 5.9 shows the operations module connecting the company's processes, activities, assets and constituents (customers and employees). A future version of the model of the company's operations will also provide NationJet with customer and employee value.

In the operations module they used a value decomposition tree, of which a simplified version is shown in Figure 5.4.

The biggest challenge to NationJet's value modeling team was developing the operations model. At first, the modeling team did not understand how to integrate customer and employee value attributes into the model. They decided to bring in some outside modeling experts. The experts showed NationJet several techniques for linking attributes of customer and employee value to one another and to the business's activities, assets and revenue. Figure 5.10 shows how model elements relate.

Figure 5.9   Value Model

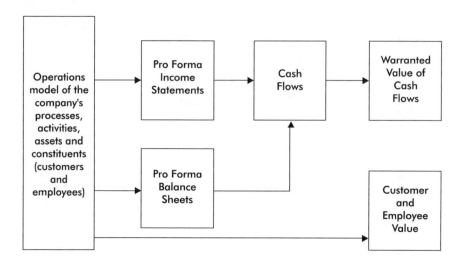

Figure 5.10 shows but a small fraction of the linkages between customer value and other key business elements. The model itself captures much more. Consider the impact of capacity and capacity utilization on employee, cus-

Figure 5.10   CVA Linkages to SVA

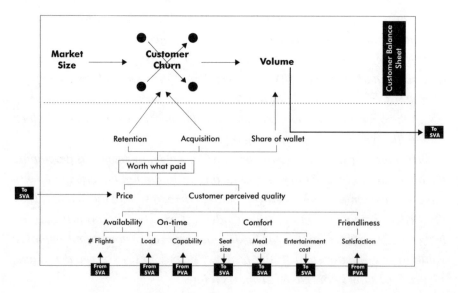

tomer and shareholder value. A company without sufficient capacity to serve its customers will experience service delays and diminishing customer-perceived quality. Insufficient capacity will place stress on employees because, like NationJet's check-in staff, they will probably be working as fast as they can to serve waiting customers, but customers who have to wait will be less pleasant to deal with. This situation can be self-correcting as discouraged customers defect to competitors, which would reduce revenue and, in term, would reduce shareholder value. If customers do not defect at a rate sufficient to bring capacity in line with demand, then employees will begin to burnout. The remaining employees will be forced to bear even larger workloads as their burned out colleagues quit or take disability leave. Diminished capacity will result in greater service delays and potentially a death spiral for the business.

The modeling team had now produced a spreadsheet model they called Domestic Airline Valuation Engine (DAVE). The first version had taken nearly three months to complete. The initial conversion of NationJet's financial model to a value model that calculated warranted value was relatively straightforward and was accomplished during the first week of the project. The development of the operations model and the incorporation of employee and customer value took considerably longer.

As he developed NationJet's model, George Braga realized that there would be no easy answers popping out, no hard-and-fast prescriptions. Modeling is comprehensive and dynamic but it doesn't offer simple explanations or categories. It is a process of precision, *as opposed to* accuracy. *Precision refers to the rigor and discipline employed in defining a relationship between two variables. Accuracy is the ability to predict outcomes. As Peter Schwartz says in* The Art of the Long View, *"The end result [of modeling and scenario planning], however, is not an accurate picture of tomorrow, but better decisions about the future."[9] The goal in modeling is precision. It is important to strive to identify the* relationships *between variables and then articulate the nature of those relationships in a rigorous and disciplined way. Modeling is not about finding the exact answer to an exact question. NationJet's value model won't explain how to fix the problem with delayed flights by increasing short turnarounds on the ramp to improve fleet utiliza-*

tion. But, and this is critically important, it will identify a causal relation between as-yet unidentified customer dissatisfaction and employee alienation. Modeling is about the relationship *between components in a company, which, in the end, sometimes turns out to be more important than the components themselves.*

Here is an example of how a value model would serve NationJet's managers when it is completed. Operating managers will be able to add inputs and watch the effect on the company's performance. By decreasing seat pitch (which translates into the amount of leg room each passenger has) they see how they can increase the number of passengers per plane and therefore potential revenue. But they can also see how customer satisfaction with the airline changes, as more disgruntled passengers get wedged into tighter spaces. NationJet learned that by adding two extra passengers to a Boeing 737, (with an average revenue increase of $350 per flight per passenger), at four flights a day, would provide about $1 million in extra revenue annually. Take away the extra operating costs of meals, extra ticketing, check-in and baggage-handling requirements of $50 a flight per passenger, and the net revenue will be only $130,000. And, by reducing the 737's seat pitch, NationJet would expect to lose 1 per cent of its overall market share, potentially eliminating any revenue gain from including those extra seats. The airline's managers saw that their decision would actually destroy value.

DAVE was a huge success at NationJet. George Braga ensured that the model was put up on the company's computer network so managers and employees could explore the model and play with it. They began to understand how various parts of the business worked together and how certain changes would impact enterprise value. It was a very exciting time. The model reinforced those strategies that were truly value creating for all stakeholders (customers, employees and shareholders). Several users found what they believed were weaknesses in the model and they brought them to the attention of the modeling team. The team was very grateful for this feedback and explained to users that there would never be a final, perfect version of DAVE. The modeling team wanted everyone to know that DAVE would continue to evolve. New versions of DAVE would be developed to reflect the company's collective advancement in its understanding of how it creates enterprise value. The interest, enthusiasm and learning generated by DAVE further encouraged NationJet's VPs to begin development of more focused models that would provide deeper insights and the value they could create from the parts of the business they oversaw. Any business can have the same exciting, rewarding experience with its own model, once it finds the tools and correct elements to make it work.

THE NATIONJET CALL CENTER: A SAMPLE DYNAMIC MODEL

The manager of NationJet's reservation department was the first to begin work on a value model for her business unit. The department was a 200-person, single-location call center that handled phone reservations and inquiries for the airline. The modeling team extracted parts of the DAVE model that were most relevant to the reservations center and then expanded detail in those areas. The team was careful not to get carried away and incorporate too much detail, recognizing that to do so would make the model overly complex and therefore incomprehensible. The completed model seemed to capture the essence of the reservation center. However, the output generated by the model did not resemble the actual patterns of performance that had been observed in the business. NationJet's modeling team did not understand the discrepancy between the model's predictions and the actual performance observed. Fortunately, the modeling experts they had called in had encountered this situation before. They pointed out that the spreadsheet model they developed for the reservation center was a typical static model. It assumed that interactions among model elements took place at the same point in time, which was really not the case for the reservation center. The modeling team recognized that there were many instances where there were delays or lags between actions and their effects. The spreadsheet they were using could not easily incorporate these lags. So the team turned to the experts for an alternative approach and tools.

The experts introduced the reservation center modeling team to systems dynamics, which the modeling team studied before returning to modeling the reservation center. This time they employed system dynamics modeling tools to build the value model. Figures 5.11 through 5.13 are schematics that show the development of the system dynamics model for the reservations center.

Figure 5.11 The Time Pressure/Efficiency Balancing Loop

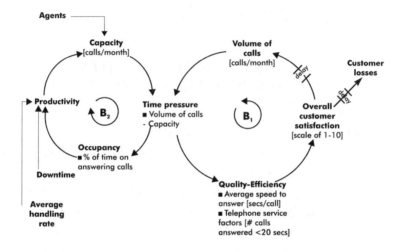

Figure 5.12 The "Burn out"/Employee Satisfaction Reinforcing Loop

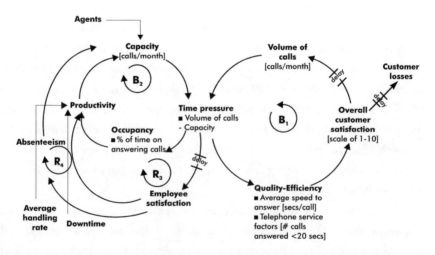

The team first drew systems dynamics models as causal loop maps, in which an arrow between two items indicates that a change in the initial element causes a change in the attached element. In combination these causal linkages create feedback loops. There are two kinds of loops, reinforcing loops and balancing loops. Reinforcing loops (also known as amplifying loops) are the drivers of accelerating growth. For example, increased spending on marketing leads to increased sales, which leads to more money for marketing expenditures, and so on. These loops also work in the opposite direction. If cash is tight, then marketing expenditures are cut back and sales drop, so cash is even tighter and so on. The loop can be driven in either direction. Balancing loops (also known as stabilizing loops) drive a system toward a specific goal. The best example is a household thermostat. As the temperature drops, the thermostat turns on the furnace, causing the temperature to rise. When the temperature reaches the desired point, the thermostat turns the furnace off, and the temperature begins to drop. Depending upon the efficiency of the insulation and furnace, the temperature will oscillate about the desired temperature.

The interaction of these loops produces behavior that typically cannot be predicted by merely examining a causal loop map. The model must be simulated to determine the outcome. For the NationJet Call Center, the team determined the model elements and their associated linkages.

Their preliminary causal loop map is shown in Figure 5.11. This diagram captures the main elements of the reservation system. The team discovered that the key dynamic in the reservation center is "time pressure," which is the ratio of call volume to call-volume capacity. The left-hand loop (B2) shows the factors which determine the call center's call-volume capacity. These factors include: occupancy (the percentage of time agents spend answering calls as opposed to doing other administrative activities), downtime (the time agents would be delayed or not available because of system failures), average handling rate (the average time required to handle an inquiry and complete any associated reservations), and the number of agents working in the reservation center. The right-hand loop (B1) shows factors that determine the volume of calls coming into the reservation center. These include: customer-perceived quality and efficiency of the agents, and the overall value perceived by the customer (which is also affected by price and other attributes of customer-perceived quality). The *dynamic reveals that time pressure was created whenever volume exceeded capacity. In the face of increasing time pressure, capacity is created for at least short periods of time by improving productivity. The result is a balancing effect (B2) as the capacity-volume gap is reduced and service levels are maintained.*

The modeling team added a second dynamic which revealed that a sustained high level of productivity leads to burnout (see Figure 5.12). Burnout results in a decline in productivity, growth in absenteeism and, ultimately, diminished capacity. A reinforcing effect (R3 and R4) is set up as the capacity-volume gap widens leading to increased time pressure and a further reduction in employee satisfaction.

This iterative development continues with the addition of further dynamic loops. The result of adding these dynamics is illustrated in Figure 5.13 below.

- *The third dynamic shows the relationship between customer satisfaction, call volume and employee satisfaction. As reduced customer*

Figure 5.13   The NationJet Call Center Model

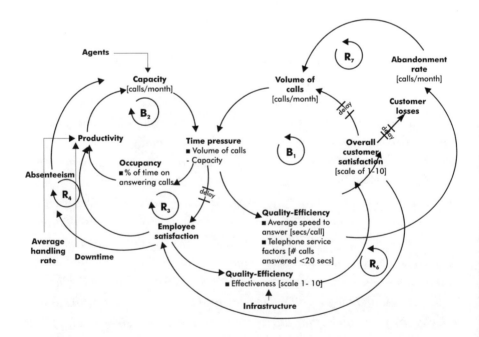

satisfaction results in business lost to competitors and a corresponding decline in call volume, reducing the capacity-volume gap and, with some delay, improving employee satisfaction, the reinforcing loop (R_3) is balanced by loop B_5.

- *The fourth dynamic captures the relationship between customer and employee satisfaction. The level of satisfaction of the customer affects employee satisfaction. If customers are satisfied, employees are happier and more effective in dealing with them, which reinforces the behavior by creating even more satisfied customers (R_6).*

- *The fifth dynamic adds the relationship between the level of efficiency and the abandoned call rate (R_7). As the efficiency and quality of the agents increases, less calls are abandoned and the volume of calls processed increases.*

- *The sixth dynamic built into the model is not related to a specific loop. This dynamic captures shocks to either the reservation center's capacity or to the volume of calls. This dynamic relates to a misleading NationJet advertisement that increased the volume of incoming calls. This rapid increase in call volume was not met by an increase in call answering capacity and resulted in a large number of abandoned calls and unhappy customers.*

The modeling team also evaluated other shocks such as prolonged failures of the reservations support systems or diminished effectiveness of these systems resulting from upgrades and changes to the system.

Next Steps for the NationJet Models

The manager of the reservation center was very excited about the system dynamics model, which produced results that closely matched the actual performance of the center. The model helped her team develop new insights about how the reservation center creates value. She was aware that her colleagues had similar models and suggested to the modeling team that they consider replacing DAVE with a super model that would integrate all the business unit models. The team was intrigued with her suggestion and dis-

cussed the idea with the modeling experts. The modeling team concluded that the super model idea was not impossible, but would represent a huge challenge. Integrating all the business-unit models would be an enormous undertaking. Moreover, the super model would be so complex that it would take a very long time to test and validate.

Nevertheless, the manager and the modeling team recognized the importance of sharing the lessons from each business unit across the business. The modeling team offered three ways to share integrated lessons. The first was to ensure the enterprise-wide model is updated to reflect significant revelations from each area of the business. Second, the team suggested the business units share their discoveries over NationJet's computer network. Third was to hold workshops where business units could share their value models and insights and discuss how various scenarios would affect each of NationJet's business units and processes.

The sharing of lessons across the NationJet business units was an important element in building the shared understanding of how the enterprise can create value. George Braga strongly supported the modeling team's recommendation for a series of workshops, and became actively involved in promoting attendance at the workshops through his weekly newsflash, and by facilitating several workshops himself. Through these efforts he was successful in creating the communications links necessary to build an understanding of how value is created and to break down the functional silos within NationJet. In his overall plan, however, this was only the first of many steps. His subsequent steps were to take the mindset and tools developed through modeling and integrate them into the definitions of operational performance measures and especially into his vision for the new planning process.

As the NationJet experience indicates, value modeling develops management's existing "mental models" of how the organization creates value into consistent, shared and explicit mental models that incorporate a value-based perspective. These shared value models help management understand the value impact of business decisions and enable them to focus on areas that have significant leverage on value, thus encouraging value-creating actions and behaviors. These mental models are captured using modeling tools as simple as spreadsheets and as complex as systems dynamics modeling tools to create a value model. The value model is then tailored to the organization and used to facilitate communication of the shared value models, the learning process and ongoing decision making.

Value modeling provides management with an understanding of the value levers and risks that have the most significant impact on value. The exercise typically refutes some long-standing heuristics and challenges managers to do things differently. With this understanding managers can assess the sensitivity of operational factors, appraise business plans and test the impact of strategic directions, all with an eye to creating enterprise value.

To truly make value the mission, modeling must evolve from a one-time exercise to an ongoing, iterative process, in which the journey of development and the organizational learning experienced along the way is as important as reaching the final destination. As we've stressed repeatedly, the process of developing value models is an exercise in learning, understanding and communicating how the elements of a business interact to create value. The most successful way is to integrate the mindset and tools throughout the management process: exploring value creating strategies and tactics, defining performance measures and evolving the compensation system.

Nevertheless, having a model doesn't solve the overlooked and underlying problems of an organization. With value models and value creating plans in place, the next challenge becomes managing and implementing the changes and ensuring that value is actually created. As all good managers know, what gets measured gets managed, and this leads us to the next phase of the Value Journey.

Chapter 6

VALUE DRIVERS AND PERFORMANCE MEASURES

Focusing on Everything is Focusing on Nothing

Now that senior management at NationJet had a value model with which to identify how value is created, they could begin testing meaningful operating parameters. But when the airline's vice presidents received the results of their value-committed CEO's probing, they were in for some head-scratching surprises.

With the help of a solid modeling team, CEO George Braga had created models for the airline's two strategic business units – the passenger and cargo divisions. Unlike the traditional schism within the corporate structure, the models cut across the traditional operations, sales and marketing organization structures and attitudes. Braga had used the model to identify what the airline should be doing in its passenger division. As mentioned in Chapter Five, NationJet had a significant corporate commitment to customer satisfaction, and its "Customer First" program was a major priority. The program was the result of extensive surveys that showed that passengers expect quality in the following areas: routing, on-time service, comfort, friendliness and safety.

After running his value model, Braga told his vice presidents that they should be cutting the quality of the meals served to economy-class passengers and raising prices for business-class travelers. The vice presidents thought that Braga was completely mad and told him that the customers need to be kept happy at all costs. Passengers tell the airline this day after day. The vice presidents couldn't see how the CEO was going to create value by reducing service levels in economy (a segment in which they had been losing market share) and raising fares for its lucrative preserve of business travelers (a segment which beat that of rival Budget Airways). Indeed, they presented Braga with evidence that over the past five years, service improvements had mitigated the airline's loss of market share.

But despite their evidence and the commendable commitment to taking care of customers, the vice presidents learned that they were wrong and their boss was right. In this instance, real value for the company would indeed come from cutting service to one segment and boosting prices in the other.

Value-Based Drivers

The reason for this is that Braga's value model had uncovered NationJet's *value drivers*. Such drivers come in two forms: *value levers* and *value risks*. Value drivers are often mentioned in organizations without a clear under-standing of what they are. Value drivers are those parameters that have an impact on the outcome of the business in terms of value created or destroyed. Value models establish the relationship between inputs and outputs. Levers can be controlled directly; risk factors cannot. If a lever is not directly con-trollable, then it's really not a lever. Employee morale, for example, is not a lever, as it cannot be directly controlled. It is a measure for which a target can be set and the achievement against that target assessed. The levers that can be controlled to influence it are things like compensation and benefits, training, challenging work, job stability and so forth.

It is essential to understand the relationship between the value levers and value risks. With a little instruction, a company can identify its own value dri-vers and measure them. When value modeling is done correctly, a company can begin to gauge the magnitude of value driver impacts that, as was the case at NationJet, will sometimes reveal some very surprising but effective results.

A company must identify what determines value in its organization and measure those things that lead to value creation. Selecting performance mea-sures is probably one of the most talked-about operational issues in business today. The need for a comprehensive conceptual model is critical because of the huge number of potential measures. The ability to boil down the multitude of possible measures to those few things that are truly the value drivers is imperative to effectively managing a value enterprise. Once enterprise value is accepted as the key outcome measure of business performance, a value model provides the capability to assess consistently the relative importance of business elements and relationships so that the key drivers can be identified.

Since the overriding goal of value-based management is to understand how every action in a business affects enterprise value, a company's goal should be to learn how to measure the impact of changes in its operating parameters. When pinpointing value drivers, tests can be made to determine which specific operating functions will have the most improvement on enterprise value, dictating where to focus energy and resources. This process is known as *sensitivity analysis*. By running scenarios and varying parameter settings featuring different assumptions about the operating environment through the value model, a company can identify the key factors that drive value in its business and measure their impact. It is universal in every business that behavior is influenced by the things that get measured. When a business and its operational parameters are identified and measured, the natural focus is on what is important. A company will want to measure what drives value.

Value-model analysis centers on discovering pragmatic value drivers from meaningful operating parameters, not from financial numbers. Many value programs recognize only a few common generic drivers as the benchmarks for uncovering value:

- Revenue
- Operating margins
- Working capital
- Asset productivity

But the trouble is that these do not lead to a value-adding plan of action. They too are the outcomes of many things that are so entangled with one another that they serve no purpose in managing for value. Not only do these generic drivers not lead to value-adding plans of action, but also it is unclear what their connection is to day-to-day operational decision making. Ideally, value drivers are independent variables that are not generalized. They can be influenced by direct managerial action. They are specific to a business and to the climate in which they are assessed. They can range from employee morale to attributes of customer-perceived quality, to wages per hour relative to employee retention, and many other factors. Once a company has run scenarios through its value model, it will begin to find the value drivers that are specific to its organization.

Just as the vice presidents in the NationJet example had intuitive feelings on what will have huge impacts on the airline's value creation, so do many of the managers we have consulted. The NationJet executives knew that they wanted to improve asset productivity, in their case fleet utilization, by keeping their aircraft in the air longer. So they shortened the turnaround times at airport ramps — the period that ground crew have to service a plane, take off inbound, and load outbound baggage. They believed, and logically so, that boosting fleet utilization would create value.

But when their ideas are run through the model, very often the impacts are minimal or even counterproductive. These are good managers, but what accounts for their judgment not producing results? Is it their overlooking of important linkages? Determining value drivers is always a matter of understanding the linkage between marketplace demand, the company's activities, and the capital being invested. Only when a manager is truly clear on these relationships, which emerge from value modeling and sensitivity analysis, is it possible to identify the value drivers needed to create a grounded and measured approach. Understanding the operational linkages is especially tricky when these linkages become apparent only over time. Benefits often lag investments, so they may be difficult to capture. When done correctly, however, the most effective value-creating images jump off the page.

An example of this stems from the telecommunications industry. The value drivers are significantly different in the long-distance and local-product lines. A simple decomposition of revenue highlights the following example (Figure 6.1).

Increasing the length of long-distance calls is a desired outcome referred to as stimulation. Getting customers to talk longer is a desired outcome of managing value levers such as advertising, ease of use, price and other factors as illustrated in Figure 6.1.

Figure 6.1   Long Distance

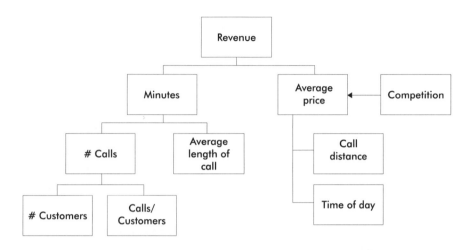

Contrast that driver with the local-exchange telecom provider (see Figure 6.2).

As the length of local calls rises — for example, as a result of increased time spent by people such as Internet users logged onto service providers — network demand, and the cost of service, increases as illustrated in Figure 6.2.

Figure 6.2   Local Calls

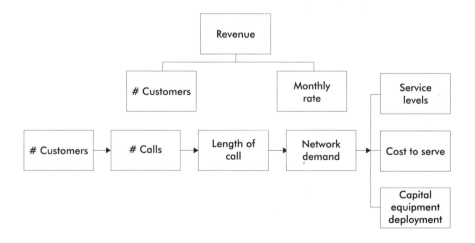

Service performance often falls significantly and capital equipment costs increase. Because local connection rates are fixed and universal service is required, an increase in call length actually destroys value. Thus one can expect local-exchange providers to press their regulators for price relief to accommodate this. Even within an industry, value drivers can work in opposite directions for different products, so a detailed understanding is critical.

Despite NationJet's admirable commitment to customer satisfaction, it continued to lose share in the economy-class market to Budget Airways because to these passengers, price is more important than good service. CEO George Braga used his model to run a sensitivity analysis on both economy-class and business-class passengers. He boosted meal quality by testing higher expenses for food preparation, increased the number of routes, and even added more flight attendants in each cabin. These variables are known as "direct measures of quality" (DMQs). Curiously, value declined; the cost of the improvements was higher than measurable benefits for which the customers were willing to pay. Economy travelers were too price conscious to notice.

When Braga examined the budget-traveler market in his model, he saw that price had so much influence that quality improvements were more expensive than they were worth. In fact, he discovered that the best strategy for the economy cabin was to reduce both *service and fares. And as for the business traveler, who is less concerned with price and more with service quality, when Braga ran various fares through the model, he was able to see at what point higher prices resulted in diminishing numbers of passengers and could thus set an optimal price. In this way he has refuted the vice presidents' conventional wisdom that quality of service was universally important for NationJet. Value is all about clarifying the goal, and picking the right route to get there.*

Like the work done by NationJet's CEO, any company's sensitivity analysis should search for both value drivers and their leverage. A company must test the sensitivity of enterprise value to each parameter. This ranking of value drivers then becomes a company's blueprint for where to focus its value-creating efforts. Early in the process, the large number of operating parameters can be intimidating. It may seem that there are too many to rank. Sensitivity analysis is often not easy, given that many value drivers are often dependent on other business parameters rather than independent. Most companies, however, find there are usually no more than 12 to 15 significant value drivers, and the degree of importance of others falls off sharply. A large number of operating parameters generally yields only a few that truly drive value.

Throughout the analysis, an understanding of the magnitude of the value drivers' leverage is crucial. That will enable a company to run scenarios like those of the NationJet CEO. Since a company must continuously strive to react quickly to changes in the marketplace, running plausible scenarios is a critical part of value-based management. If value drivers are consistently significant under every scenario that a company runs, then it's obvious that those are the drivers that it will have to focus on. If there are other drivers that are important in certain scenarios but unimportant in others, then the focus will probably have to be shifted and the validity of those drivers revisited if those certain scenarios materialize. And that is the important understanding to achieve. Because of the dynamics of change, a company cannot assume that drivers will remain the same. There may be times when NationJet will have to adjust its precepts about business travelers and fares, if, for example, another airline begins to target its passenger base with lower fares. With proper modeling and sensitivity analysis, a company can have dynamic, forward-looking and forecasts grounded in measurable and proven information.

There is a category of value drivers worth noting. These appear only under particular, rare scenarios, but the impact of mismanaging them is so catastrophic that it breaks the existing business model. In these situations the changes in value drivers warrant the development of new business strategies.

Here's an example from the telecommunications industry. In late 1996, America Online (AOL) offered unlimited Internet access for a flat rate. This removed the incentive for Internet users to use their time efficiently, and in some cases users would no longer log off when not using the service. As a result the average length of calls (as well as the busy signals received by AOL customers) on AOL's lines exploded. This action, and the competitive response of other Internet service providers to offer similar pricing schemes necessitated that the local exchange carrier make engineering changes to the access portion of their network delivering local services so that other customers were not affected. (The local network access is engineered to support calls averaging several minutes, not several hours.) To the local exchange carriers, this scenario, in which a change in the actions of its customers had a very large impact on a cost, capital and service level, was therefore a value driver. The magnitude of AOL's price change affected the business model of other Internet providers and local-exchange carriers almost overnight. While AOL did not invent this price scheme, its implementation was a seminal event.

Discovering value drivers is not arcane or particularly complicated. Figure 6.3 uses value models as the basis for testing the sensitivity of operating parameters by determining leverage factors. These are simply measures of how sensitive enterprise value is to a change in the operating parameter. For example, a 3 percent change in enterprise value as a result of a 1 percent change in the operating parameter implies a three to one leverage factor.

Figure 6.3   Using the Model for Sensitivity Analysis

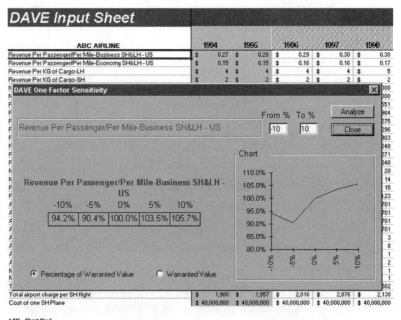

Throughout the sensitivity analysis, each parameter carries with it whatever unique relationships it has to other areas in the business, and those interrelationships are taken into consideration to a large degree in its ranking for overall value. So the model will simulate the impact of a parameter on others, inside or outside the domain of the one being tested. The goal is to understand the net effect of how much amplification or leverage resides in each operating parameter compared to others. The analysis shows the trade-offs on specific variables that will be at cross purposes with one another. Sometimes, parameters lose their value impact because of this. If they drag too many other factors in the opposite direction that ultimately run counter to value, they will end up lowering that parameter's leverage factor. The goal is to find those drivers that have the biggest and most positive impact on enterprise value. Understanding the degree to which each parameter affects value is all part of understanding where to spend time digging and where not to waste it.

Consider how George Braga arrived at his conclusion about reducing service in NationJet's economy cabins. He would have run figures through his model that reduced the amount of money spent on each passenger's meal and then looked for what changes it would have on warranted value. The attribute of meal quality is a DMQ. Suppose that NationJet's competitor, Budget Airways, were spending $4 on a passenger meal compared to NationJet's $7. Braga decreased the investment in meals by 1 percent and began to track perceived changes in customer satisfaction leading to the loss of market share and warranted value. As the quality and cost of the meal dropped customer dissatisfaction would increase, slowly at first, then accelerate. At some point, Braga would find that a meal costing, let's say, $3.75, would be so spartan that it would actually drive customers away. This impact of meal quality on warranted value is illustrated in Figure 6.4.

In a similar vein, Braga tested increases in airfares for the business-class cabin to see at what point there is a significant decrease in passenger loads. He was able to simulate the highest fare the business-class passenger will tolerate relative to the value of the service and amenities that NationJet is providing.

So, with sensitivity analysis, a company can achieve a clarification far beyond what was previously possible. The process defines the key value drivers and then reveals trade-offs between parameters. The interrelationships

Figure 6.4   Impact of Meal Quality on Value

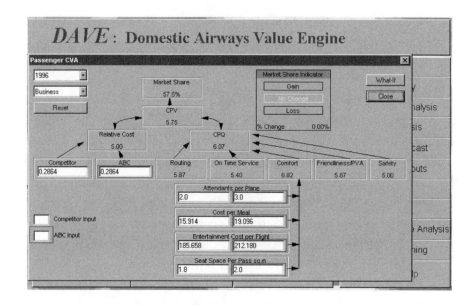

between operating parameters become obvious when the model is constructed, enabling a company to reduce the number of decisions it makes based on guesswork and hunches.

And there are many other variables that Braga and other key managers could run through the value model. By value testing a wide range of scenarios, they can identify and outline the most probable ones. When they increase wages by 1 percent, morale is improved by 4 percent. By reducing the number of flights that fly during mealtimes by 10 percent, they free up money to improve the quality of meals served on the remaining flights by a commensurate amount, but improve customer satisfaction by 5 percent. Figure 6.5 considers the leverage effect of an independent one percent change in each operational variable on warranted value.

Value Driver Characteristics

The combination of an understanding of value drivers as levers or risks along with the corresponding sensitivity information can provide valuable insights

Figure 6.5   Leverage Value of Measures

DAVE Input Sheet	Sensitivity
Avg. Miles Per Hour SH Plane [Miles]	0.953
Avg. Flight Turnaround Time Between Flights SH [HR's]	-0.496
Avg. Time: SH Flight [HR's]	0.460
Fuel Usage per Mile [litres]	-0.396
Fuel Cost Per Liter	-0.396
Total airport charge per SH flight	-0.191
Avg. Time: LH Flight [HR's]	0.142
Avg. Miles Per Hour LH Plane [Miles]	0.142
Fully loaded salary: Personnel-Technical	-0.125
Average Turnaround Maintenance Cost Per Hour - SH	-0.120
Number of technicians per SH plane	-0.109
Avg. Flight Turnaround Time Between Flights LH [HR's]	-0.103
Fully loaded salary: Personnel-Pilots	-0.076
Number of pilots per SH plane	-0.063
Average Turnaround Maintenance Cost Per Hours - LH	-0.037
Total airport charge per LH flight	-0.031
Number of technicians per LH plane	-0.016
Number of pilots per LH plane	-0.013
Average Regular Maintenance Cost Per Hours - SH	-0.002
Maintenance Time Per Month: SH [Days]	-0.002
Average Regular Maintenance Cost Per Hours - LH	0.000
Maintenance Time Per month: LH [Days]	0.000

*SH — Short Haul

LH — Long Haul

into understanding the characteristics of the value drivers. As illustrated in Figure 6.6, sensitivity analysis is used to identify the highest leverage drivers and then separate them into these two categories. Understanding the difference between value levers and value risks is critical to effectively managing value creation. Otherwise, a company risks blurring its overall picture of value creation.

The cable-television industry provides a good illustration. If a cable company with eight million subscribers raises service prices, value increases because of additional revenue without significant negative trade-offs within the company. But because cable in most countries is a regulated industry, the only the way the price of service can be increased is by regulators' decisions. So is measuring price an appropriate factor when identifying value levers in a regulated cable company? Probably not, because it will only change once a year (if at all), and price is not something over which the company has managerial control. This makes it a value risk as opposed to a value lever (that the company can control).

Figure 6.6   The Value Screen

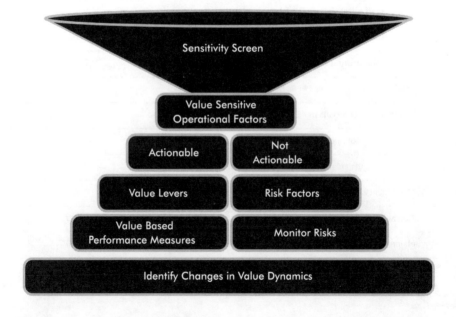

A company must not only understand what its value risks are, but also develop strategies to lessen them continually. The fact that a company does not enjoy total control over risks makes them dangerous to ignore. A business must form strategies regularly about what might be done to mitigate deterioration or lessen the company's exposure to those value risks. Even if the risks are perceived to be improbable, a company should develop alleviation strategies if those risks have significant impact on value. With the cable company example, let's assume that over time, the regulators became unreasonable in their reluctance to raise cable prices. At that point, the company's relationship with the regulator does become a value driver. Through regular constructive meetings, the company could improve its relationship with the regulator to the point that it becomes reasonable in its decisions again. But unless this action is strategically focused in a company's overall plan, it will probably get overlooked. The positive outcome of identifying value risks and value levers is that a company's strategic thinking becomes focused and specific. It now has a clear picture about what drives value and an accurate understanding of the linkages among the drivers. Only when that exists is it truly within a manager's realm to form strategy and plan effectively.

Another characteristic of value drivers are thresholds and optimal levels. For some value drivers there is a building up of effectiveness and then a point at which the effectiveness peaks: an optimal level. When Braga increases wages in his value model, he will see a point where further wage increases would yield no significant improvements in employee morale. Once that level is reached, there is a decline or a value destroying impact. Wages have a clear threshold of effectiveness if driven too high or too low. When NationJet tries cutting wages in the model, Braga must consider the impact on quality, quality's impact on demand, and ultimately, demand's impact on revenue and overall enterprise value. So cutting hourly wages is a value driver up to the point where the improvements begin to affect other variables. And the same is true of wage increases. For example, if a retail photo-processing business decides to pay an employee a higher wage because he has a degree in photography, chances are good that the knowledge he displays to the consumer about things like film, photo composition, and light levels, will pay off in repeat business. But if a high-priced photojournalist from the *New York Times* is hired to work behind the same photo counter, obviously the cost would exceed the need. The business would go beyond the optimal level for the value driver. The wage paid to the employee with the photography degree is probably the optimal level for that value driver in that particular business.

It is evident that it is not enough to just identify the value drivers in a business. Understanding a driver inside and out, and knowing its every nuance, is the goal in value-based management. All drivers are linked to enterprise value, but equally important is knowing their unique thresholds, their optimal and minimal levels, which ones carry ranges, and which ones affect trade-offs in other variables. Understanding all of this is one of the most compelling parts of the analysis. In value-based management, it is well worth figuring all this out. Effectively managing drivers is not a one-time event. Rather, as the drivers and their nuances change with market dynamics, management needs to monitor, understand, and adapt continuously. An important part of this type of analysis, is the shared learning and understanding that is acquired by managers as a result of the process. Managers share insights, which leads to improved organizational learning. Workshops where managers focus on determining and understanding value drivers are often the most important steps in a Value Journey of an organization.

Value Drivers and Performance Measures

The next step is to create performance measures from value drivers. Measures flow logically from the levers that have the greatest impact on enterprise value. The fact that they are derived from a focus deep within the processes of a company's operations means that they are broadly representative of the organization. Every company in business measures performance by holding employee reviews and generally trying to get people's performance aligned with some unifying link to an overall company or department strategy. The goal is to be able to sit down with an employee and define what clear and demonstrable things he or she has brought to the company in relation to the overall strategy. Logically, value-based management advocates taking the value drivers in an organization and linking them to the institutional parts of the company that deal with performance. It's impossible to redefine all performance measures overnight, so the real-world goal should be to work within the company's existing framework to get the value drivers nested into performance measurement. In this way, an employee's annual review would include assessment of his performance in the areas which are the company's significant value drivers. Through this method, an employee's performance can be assessed relative to his peers, as well as relative to creating value for the company.

Determining the right measures can be incredibly complex given the multitude of cause and effect impacts. Call centers, for example, collect a huge amount of information that might be considered performance measures: calls per employee, call duration, absenteeism, speed to answer, and customer satisfaction to name a few. A focus on specific measures will drive behavior with some potentially negative impacts. An excessive focus on time spent on calls may reduce morale and increase absenteeism. Focusing on shorter call duration may reduce customer satisfaction. The point is that many potential measures have complex interrelationships that must be clearly understood from a value perspective. These relationships must be properly modeled if the right measures are to be selected and the right behaviors created.

We find that companies everywhere continually struggle with how to measure performance. And no wonder; there are so many ways to approach the procedure. Some experts advocate purely financial measures; others subscribe to nonfinancial and quality-based, customer-related or even process-related measurements. Still others say there should be a balance of all of these things when employee performance is assessed. Popular value programs advocate traditional finance-based performance measures such as economic profit revenue, operating margin, working capital and asset productivity. The problem is that all these are strictly financial in nature, and as previously indicated, they do not point to value-enhancing action. If operating managers are told to improve asset productivity or operating margins, what exactly does that mean? Do they specifically know what actions to take to achieve the improvement? Probably not, because that financial measure is an outcome of many factors that are inextricably linked. A single manager rarely has control over all the factors linked to asset productivity or improving operating margins.

Many approaches also confuse outcomes with determinants. Typically, historical financial measures are outcome measures, how well a company did, but say nothing about how to do better in the future. To get a better understanding of potential performance, it is necessary to understand the levers and risks and the possible scenarios associated with them. The value enterprise puts far more emphasis on the lead measures than the historical outcomes or lag measures. Value-based management is about large windshields and small rearview mirrors.

One of the most popular approaches today is to create a balanced set of measures including both financial and nonfinancial items. While nonfinancial measures are more often relevant to operational managers, most methods offer no conceptual basis for measure selection other than intuition. Traditional methods do not link the financial impact of changes in the operational measures, so there is no way to determine relative importance. Given the potentially staggering number of possible measures, this creates a significant problem in selecting the most appropriate measures for an organization.

Through the exercises of modeling, sensitivity analysis and identifying value drivers, some very robust and empowering information is created. Great care is taken to emphasize that only a limited number of factors matter in the management domain and only a limited number are under an employee's control. So how could one logically ask someone to be responsible for the performance of something out of their control? In the resource industry, for example, financial performance is heavily influenced by commodity prices and environmental regulations, something over which local managers have no control. To create accountability, performance measures must factor out uncontrollable variables in order to separate good luck from good management.

Our method of linking value drivers to performance, rewards managers for the direct influence they exercise over things that are known to create value. The practical elements identified as value drivers are the primary measures that should be linked to performance measures. But how can this be accomplished in an existing institutional framework? What makes this task particularly difficult is the fact that many organizations are functionally organized and the value drivers will result from a process perspective. So it is often hard to manage for value within current organizational boundaries.

A value driver approach begins with finding out what is beyond a company's averages by observing the peaks and valleys of its business in each division. This enables a company to delineate a range of corporate performance. The goal is to determine the "best of breed" for each functional area of operation. Through modeling, a company's operating parameters and value drivers have already been defined and in many cases, performance averages may already reside within that information. For a hamburger chain it might be the number of hamburgers and french fry orders processed per cook. For a retail photo lab it could be the rolls of new film sold with each processed order picked up. For a car dealership, it might be the number of cars and warranty contracts sold per salesperson each month. A company must first look internally to build the range of performance, then establish the averages, and finally determine the best of breed. An extremely driven target level of performance is important.

The next step is to consider the external world. By identifying value drivers, a company can learn where it should focus to create value. Unfortunately, it has no way of knowing what its standard should be. How does one know what targets to establish? To find out, a company must look at its peers. With insight into what competitors are doing, it is possible to set targets more accurately. If an automobile dealership thinks its goal for a car salesmen is 100 cars a year with 50 warranty contracts, but its competitor's is 200 sales with 100 warranty contracts, it must find out why. Is their objective higher because of something environmental, something to do with the location perhaps, or is it performance based? Maybe their salesmen have administrative assistants to process all the paperwork while the other company's staff does their own. The simple process of finding the answers to these questions provides crucial information for staying competitive as well as giving real depth to a company's performance measures, which in turn results in truly motivating the workforce.

Once a company understands through modeling what its business drivers are, it will know what to manage. How does it set targets? By focusing on the best internal practices and the best of its industry's. With value models, a company can test the targets and see what their effect will be on value. This will help calibrate the targets (maybe best of breed is not good enough to create value). Similarly, initiatives for process improvements can be tested to see if the improvement is worth the cost of getting there. A company should look to the future, not be the best of someone else's yesterday, but be the best of tomorrow.

Chapter 7

VALUE-BASED COMPENSATION

Getting What you Pay For

In June 1996 the Levi Strauss Company announced a plan to reward each of its 37,500 employees worldwide with a one-time bonus equal to one year's pay if the company met its performance goals over the next six years. Company chairman Robert D. Haas summed up the corporate philosophy, "Motivated employees are our source of innovation and competitive advantage. By acknowledging and rewarding their efforts, we not only demonstrate our appreciation but also encourage them to continue striving for new standards of excellence."[1] For employees to receive the full bonus, the company must achieve a "cumulative cash flow" of $7.6 billion by November 2001, a goal company officials expect to exceed. The $7.6 billion target, compared to the $1.09 billion in cash flow the clothing maker had in 1995, refers to cumulative earnings before interest, taxes, depreciation and amortization. This pretax operating cash flow is clearly a good value measure for them. When growth is factored in, it is not unrealistic that the targeted goal will be met, and each employee will receive an extra year's pay. This is quite an incentive plan by anyone's standard.

Levi Strauss has a reputation for progressive human resources policies. In 1992, for example, it became the first *FORTUNE 500* company to offer full medical benefits to all unmarried partners of its employees. But the incentive plan caught even union officials off guard, "We were flabbergasted when the company came around and said they wanted to share the wealth," Frank

Nicholas, a vice president of the Union of Needle Trades, Industrial and Textile Employees, told the *Los Angeles Times*.[2] The 145-year-old company realized its gesture would reap goodwill but would also translate into huge value creation.

The Levi Strauss approach is hard not to love. It represents clearheaded wisdom about tying compensation to real value creation.

One of the keys to making the value enterprise a reality lies in linking employee compensation to value creation. Some argue that this should be the first step in the journey, not the last. The logic in this view is that people will get turned on by the possibility of increasing their wealth and will therefore invest the time and money in taking the steps required to achieve their performance targets. This is a dangerous step, however, if people in the company do not have a clear understanding of how they can contribute to enterprise value.

We have seen several disastrous situations where financial reward plans created extreme and bizarre behavior because they were not fully thought out or where education on value creation and desired behavior was inadequate. Linking compensation to the performance measures described in Chapter Six will reinforce the effort to focus attention on the company's value drivers and is a powerful motivation that can accelerate the Value Journey. Also, if the power of the value enterprise is to be achieved, all employees must ultimately share in the value that is created.

Traditionally, most organizations have considered compensation as purely an expense item, simply a cost of doing business. Value-based management, however, strives to broaden the picture by demonstrating that people are the very source of value creation. They are the one sustainable resource that every business has, and without them, it is virtually impossible to create value. Therefore, employees should be managed as a company asset and should be the beneficiaries of a company-wide attitude that sees compensation as a function of each individual's contribution to value creation, regardless of rank or level in the company.

The Link to Performance Measures

The overall goal should be to create an environment in which the remuneration system is consistent with what drives value in the company. Employees should understand and acknowledge that the creation of value, and their contribution to it, is the very thing that delivers the paychecks they take home. In Chapter Six we stated that to focus on everything is to focus on nothing; here, we can say that what gets paid for gets done. Even for those employees whose hard work is motivated by factors other than the compensation system, the value-based incentive compensation plan will reinforce where the focus of effort belongs. It is therefore essential to select a few drivers and behavior that will create the most value for the enterprise. When viewed as a tool for creating a value culture in lieu of payment for work, compensation can become a significant point of leverage for a company.

Employees and management represent the frontline constituency that truly creates value. It is only logical that their rewards should be aligned with the degree to which they carry out their roles. Since they are the primary creators of value, they should be encouraged and compensated based on their ability to do so. As obvious as this seems, few companies have incentives that are actually linked to value creation. That's because incentives are either geared to the earnings perspective or there are none at all. Compensation that gets tied to annual financial results generally encourages managers to focus on making the present year look good without considering future, long term outcomes. As has been pointed out in other chapters, annual financial results are not pure value performance measures because they are encumbered by many factors that one person alone cannot control. As such, they are not effective value levers.

Figure 7.1 shows a Conference Board of New York study of the performance measures used by companies in determining compensation. Note that accounting measures dominate the list. Cash flow and economic profit rank at the bottom. But it is encouraging that total shareholder return was reported by a reasonable number of respondents as a commonly used standard for employee remuneration. As the Conference Board noted, this indicates that "companies [appear to be] moving away from traditional accounting-based performance criteria to use more comprehensive tools for strategic decision making."

Figure 7.2 identifies the financial performance measures most commonly used to determine executive compensation in the top 100 of the *FORTUNE 500* companies. Again, accounting measures dominate the list.

Figure 7.1   Corporate Financial Performance Measures in the
United States

(N = 149)

Performance Measures	Number Reporting
Earnings per share	38
Return on equity	36
Earnings	30
Return on assets	16
Revenue	13
Total shareholders return	13
Return on invested capital	8
Return on sales	5
Market share	2
Operating income	2
Cash flow	1
Economic profit	1
Equity growth	1
Net worth growth	1

Note:
Participants could report more than one measure.

Source: Long Term Unit/Share Programs, The Conference Board, New York, Report #1114-95-RR, 1995, p. 12
Reprinted by permission.

But Figure 7.3 indicates an emerging trend toward more nonfinancial performance measures for determining executive compensation.

The Nature of Compensation

In any discussion of compensation, it is important to understand its relationship to risk. We traditionally associate risk with investing, not something to do with employees. With every movement in the market, a shareholder's money is at risk. To help counter that risk, traditional financial strategy has always included diversification so that an investor's money is not exposed to just one area. But risk is also part of the reward picture for employees at all levels, and it is inconsistent to apply the strategy of diversification to an employee's

Figure 7.2   Financial Measures Used to Determine Executive Compensation in the Top 100 Fortune 500 Companies

Performance Measures[1]	% of Companies Using This Measure
Net income	32%
Pretax profit	23
Operating profit	16
Economic profit[2]	1
Return on equity	37
Earnings per share	29
Return on assets	19
Return on capital employed	6
Revenue	20
Cash flow	12
Working capital	5
Cost reduction	13
Inventory	2
Receivables	1
Stock price appreciation	27

Note:
[1]   Companies may use more than one measure to set compensation.
[2]   The total cost of the company's or business unit's capital. Variable pay is based on year-to-year improvements.

Source: Marc-Andreas Klein, Top Executive Pay for Performance, The Conference Board, Report # 1113-95-RR, 1995, p. 15
        Reprinted by permission.

salary. Most employees work for one company and earn one paycheque, and their fate rides with whatever happens to that company. An employee's pay cannot be put at great risk because he has no ability to diversify or offset an unacceptable level of exposure to loss. This basic fact must be considered when building compensation strategies.

There are basically three types of employee pay and each has a level of risk attached to it: wealth at risk, pay at risk and raise at risk. The highest is wealth at risk, which has the greatest impact at the executive level, because executives often have ownership in the company, sometimes in the form of

Figure 7.3   Non-financial Performance Measures Used to Determine Executive Compensation in the Top 100 Fortune 500 Companies

Performance Measures	% of Companies Using This Measure
Organization and business development[1]	27%
Stakeholder interests[2]	27
Quality	25
Customer satisfaction	24
New product development	23
Market share	10
Workplace issues[3]	10
Ethics	5
Corporate performance	50
Individual and business unit performance	49

Note:
[1] Divestiture, restructuring, rationale of capital expenditure, business planning process, team management, (management strategies).
[2] Public affairs, civic involvement, environmental issues.
[3] Workforce diversity, people development, high-performance workplace.

Source: Marc-Andreas Klein, Top Executive Pay for Performance, The Conference Board, Report # 1113-95-RR, 1995, p. 16
    Reprinted by permission.

share-purchase loans. Other employees may also have equity in the company through special stock-purchase programs. The fate of the company and its market performance has direct impact on employee wealth. The next level is pay at risk. This is an amount of pay that is tied to some kind of incentive. The worst-case scenario with this level of risk would be if an employee met none of the incentive criteria and realized only his base pay. The third and lowest level is raise at risk. This means that from year to year employees are informed of what their salary will be, and that any raise in the next year is based on performance. The worst-case scenario here is that no raise will be given and the employee will simply continue to earn the same amount as the previous year.

Figure 7.4   Median Compensation

CEO's	1991	1993
Annual bonus as a percent of base pay	70.2%	89.9%
Restricted stock as a percent of base pay	76.1	88.0
Long-term incentive plans as a percent of base pay	54.4	80.5

Source: Marc-Andreas Klein, Top Executive Pay for Performance, The Conference Board, Report # 1113-95-RR, 1995, p. 19
      Reprinted by permission.

The biggest problem with compensation today is not with the much-discussed dizzying executive awards. It lies in the fact that incentive compensation remains largely the preserve of senior executives, where it is growing as a percentage of overall income, as can be seen in Figure 7.4.

Incentive-focused compensation is also growing as a percentage for other employees but not to the same significant degree. A Conference Board study found that less than 1 percent of companies surveyed provide significant long-term incentive plans for most of their employees and that less than 4 percent offer stock options to most of their employees. Figure 7.5 shows the frequency of different compensation types by level of employment.

Figure 7.5   Frequency of Compensation Type by Level

	Executives	Senior Managers	Managers	Employees
Base salary	X	X	X	X
Annual bonus	X	X	□	□
Restricted stock	□	O	O	O
Stock options	□	□	□	□
Long-term incentive plans	□	O	O	O

Legend:
X = Most employees within this level receive this form of compensation
□ = Some employees within this level receive this form of compensation
O = Few employees within this level receive this form of compensation

For most, their sole income is base pay, which means their compensation is not tied to value creation, yet they represent the largest group contributing to an organization's value. The equation is backward. Corporations spend too much time today imparting group leadership plans and programs with the intent of improving company value, but these efforts often fail because the mandate and incentives for the very people expected to carry them out is typically inadequate. It is obvious that if middle management and lower-ranking employees don't use the plans company leaders mastermind, the value creation will not occur. Clearly, there are many more managers and employees who could play a significant role in value creation if their compensation plans reinforced the right mandate and created the right incentives.

The old, established methods of compensation often have little effect on creating value, and sometimes they can be even counterproductive. When it comes to senior management, base pay is shrinking as the dominant form of financial reward, as you would expect since investors increasingly expect executive pay to be tied to performance. Bonuses and long-term performance plans that reward good corporate performance make up a bigger portion of compensation. This is beginning to spread to lower organizational levels.

But there is a problem with traditional annual bonuses. In most companies the annual bonus is really treated like base pay, and has become as much a part of expected earnings as the weekly paycheck. Too many companies peg bonuses to surprisingly modest performance, virtually guaranteeing them. Only a small percentage of the total bonus is actually tied to measures and targets that represent any serious growth or corporate improvement. Some companies tie bonuses to measures that are not really measures of performance at all. One firm tied much of its bonus plan to customer satisfaction, which was so subjective as to be meaningless: customers responding to bonus-determining surveys were chosen by the sales reps receiving the bonuses!

Other long-term compensation programs such as restricted stock or share unit incentives represent an alternative to stock options. Long-term incentive plans usually provide a cash or stock award for realizing performance targets over several years, such as in the Levis Strauss example. Some companies have replaced stock options with these long-term incentive plans, which can be tied to performance measures over which employees enjoy significant influence. Favorable tax treatment and fluctuating stock markets have driven a 20-year trend to increasing such long-term pay tools. Restricted stock, often nicknamed "golden handcuffs," are shares granted usually to an executive and subject to restrictions against their sale or transaction for a period of usually one to five years. Because the recipient cannot sell their stock, it ensures performance motivation and loyalty to the firm. Unfortunately, once the no-sale period ends, the golden handcuffs come off and restricted shares are no longer relevant as performance incentives.

Even traditional stock options have a dubious role in driving value creation. Still the most popular form of long-term variable pay, stock options became popular with boards of directors and compensation departments because they thought they provided effective links between executive pay and company performance. But recently that link has grown questionable. It's common for stock-option holders to gain significant benefits during rising stock markets, even if their firm's actual performance hasn't matched it. As the saying goes, "a rising tide lifts even leaky boats." In bull markets the reward is often disproportionate to company performance. This is at the core of the current controversy over huge CEO remuneration. Conversely, in a bear market, even good performance will not stop compensation from eroding, as happened in the 1970s. It was exactly such a situation that prompted the growth of long-term incentives.

You would think that currently popular long-term incentives would instill a sense of the long term value that shareholders crave, but not always. One leading consulting firm found that most companies believe that their current compensation schemes fail to elicit the right results in performance, behavior and outcomes. Many of these companies believe that their incentive programs are not tied to the right levers but rather to accounting measures or stock options.

Typically, long-term incentives are cash or shares, given in consecutive annual grants, overlapping one another, depending on specific objectives and performance standards. If performance falls below a threshold, there is no payment. Above that there are gradations. For example, if performance relative to target is partial, perhaps 50 percent of the plan is payable. If the highest criteria are achieved, the executive receives 100 percent, or even more. Companies may use benchmarks to determine performance relative to their industry. The problem with such plans is that it is usually restricted to top executives. It is often argued that they are the only ones to significantly affect corporate financial performance. We emphatically disagree. As you will see later in this chapter, long-term incentives tied to value creation should be a facet of *every* employee's compensation.

There is also difficulty with the proportion of bonuses to total financial reward. Redefining that proportion would help prevent executives from making short-term corporate performance look good (such as by deferring R&D or capital investments), then leaving for another job in a different company without having created long-term value. Finally, senior management compensation should not be tied to accounting measures. While there is an emerging trend toward more value-based numbers, such as cash flow and total shareholder return, far too many plans rely on traditional accounting figures. If management is to align its interests with that of corporate value creation, accounting numbers should not be used. Gauges must be value-based.

Key Principles

Since value-based management looks to the future to maximize enterprise value, compensation schemes should reflect those characteristics. Value-based compensation measures introduced to human resources departments are often met with doubts about how employees can be motivated to create value when they do not understand their role in its creation. It is precisely in those situations that value-based compensation can have the most impact. The very notion that a company has people who do not understand how they contribute to value creation should be unacceptable to any business. Yet this is indeed the case in a vast majority of firms, and in fact is the very reason why the whole concept of value-based management came about. Only when people understand their role in an organization and clearly perceive how they can contribute to value, is value creation going to take place on any significant scale. It only makes sense, then, to encourage value-creating behavior with value-based rewards.

When it comes to implementing practical value-based compensation, options are unlimited. The main object is to be creative but stay focused on this rule: you get what you pay for. There are four principles that should guide your plans:

1. They should be aligned with the performance of individual employees, the team, the division and the company. In other words, compensation should not be strictly a function of individual performance measures, but must also consider how success in one area of the company will play across the entire business. This is critical since there are natural interconnections across the business that must be optimized.

2. Incentives for individual employees should be tied to performance measures that they can influence and control. Value drivers are the most relevant measures because, through modeling, a company goes to great lengths to define the value drivers for each area of its business. The next logical step is to set performance targets for the drivers. A performance target must be an achievable stretch, requiring some real effort and perhaps innovation, and not falling into the guaranteed bonus category.

3. Incentive bonuses should be banked in the "bonus bank" with scaled annual withdrawals. A bonus bank encourages a longer-term commitment from employees, who are more likely to remain with the company to collect their bonus. When a bonus is awarded, it would be put in an individual bonus bank with annual withdrawals limited to no more than one-third the total balance. What this allows for is the averaging of the bonus payment so that if an employee had a good year and then a bad year and then another good year, he would not feel the full impact of the oscillation in any one year.

4. The percentage of pay at risk and length of bonus bank withdrawals should be relative to rank in the organization. Typically, the further up in the organization, the higher the bonus is as a percentage of the total reward. The percentage of pay at risk can be higher with higher compensation levels because the tolerance for risk goes up as total pay goes up. Similarly, because senior management is responsible for the longer term, the bonus bank withdrawal period should also be longer.

Value-based compensation must not be strictly a function of individual performance measures, but rather one of individuals trying to understand how they contribute to their sphere of influence, as well as to the success of the business as a whole. Accordingly, performance bonuses should be based on a mix of performance targets at different levels in the organization. The goal is to have employee earnings rise and fall with overall performance.

The Value-Based Incentive Framework

In order to establish this comprehensive, across-the-board plan, it is necessary to set up an incentive framework that supplements the base pay. The main elements of a value-based incentive framework are: overall business performance, bonus targets and performance relative to targets. Let's examine each of these in detail.

Overall business performance uses comprehensive measures of value created by the enterprise: customer value, employee value and shareholder value. Specific targets for overall business performance are established for each of the major business scenarios. The overall business performance targets are associated with performance targets for value drivers that exist at the level of individuals, teams and divisions.

Many companies face potential major events that would have a significant impact on business performance. Often they set compensation targets that end up based on a presumed outcome of events that fails to happen. Companies should identify the major potential courses of action that could affect performance, then establish appropriate targets, thresholds, and performance levels for each of them. In this way, it is possible to get around the dangerous game of trying to predict what kind of major events might affect a business.

Bonus targets represent incentive compensation for individuals, provided all performance targets are met by the individual, his or her team, the division or business unit and the company as a whole. The amount of bonus target, or pay at risk, should be relative to the individual's rank or level in the organization. Higher ranking individuals would probably get greater pay at risk, while risk for lower ranking individuals would diminish with their level in the organization. These targets are established at each level and will be awarded if the agreed performance is achieved.

Performance relative to targets is an assessment of actual performance relative to planned performance for the measures agreed at each of the individual, team and business unit levels. Since value drivers have already been identified through value modeling, this step involves the specific measures and targets for individual employees, teams and the division as a whole. The idea is to encourage individuals to do those things that they alone can affect, while at the same time establishing performance targets for both teams and divisions. These should always be achievable and realistic, otherwise employees will be discouraged from trying to reach the desired level of performance. "Stretch targets," which not easily achieved, should be the basis for any long-term incentive plan. A long-term incentive plan should include a threshold, below which no bonus is paid, a target performance level at which 100 percent of the bonus is realized and then a superb performance level above which a premium is paid on the bonus. Once established, actual performance can be assessed relative to the targets and a performance rating can be calculated.

The total bonus earned for any employee should be made up of two components: a business performance bonus and value driver bonus. The business performance bonus is made up of the business performance bonus target and the actual business performance. The value driver bonus is a function of the value driver bonus target and value driver performance. These, of course, are relative to the performance target at each level of employee, team and business unit.

Hank Anderson, NationJet's vice president of human resources, knew that his group eventually would be called upon to assist in the design of value-based compensation plans. So he decided to get an early jump on the challenge. Anderson called his colleague in charge of the reservation department and asked her to work with him on a value-based compensation plan for reservation center staff. She welcomed the idea and identified her group's business unit, team and individual value drivers and performance targets through the value airline's modeling exercise. This information would prove critical in the design of the value-based rewards plans.

The vice presidents from HR and the reservation center assigned a team to develop a value-based plan for the agents who perform telephone sales. The existing income plan for the agents was basic: they were on straight salary with ranges defined for different lengths of tenure, and received annual raises based on performance. The team recognized that the new plan would be dramatically different. The structure of the new plan would feature base pay plus incentives. The team debated how much the incentives should be as a proportion of total compensation and how to introduce the plan. Everyone agreed that the agents needed to have some skin in the game, but there were lengthy discussions about how much and how soon. Eventually, the team concluded that it would be difficult to introduce a plan that would reduce the agents' paychecks. So the team decided to set the agents' current salary levels as base pay. The annual raise would be replaced by a new incentive component that would be phased in over three years. The incentive compensation target would be 25 percent of the base pay by the end of the third year. Phasing in meant that the agents would have less pay at risk in the first year of the plan, when they were still figuring out how the plan worked. The incentive would grow with their understanding of the plan as well as their savvy in creating value.

Figure 7.6   NationJet's Incentive Compensation Plan

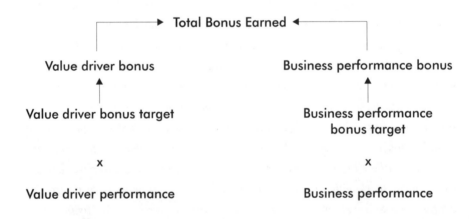

The incentive plan featured a bonus target and a performance target. The bonus target is the amount of incentive compensation that the individual will receive if he or she meets all performance targets. The performance targets consist of overall business performance targets (for customer, employee and shareholder value) and value drivers for the business unit, the team and

the individual. All the goals are achievable, stretch targets that create value for NationJet. Different targets are established for each situation. The structure for the incentive component is shown in Figure 7.6.

The team proposed a value driver bonus target of $4,500 and business performance bonus target of $2,000 in the third year. The value driver portion of the bonus is the largest because it features drivers over which the agents have considerable influence. The business performance component will ensure that the agents are motivated to do things that will help the company's overall performance.

Value driver performance would be calculated using the table featured in Figure 7.7.

Scores for specific value drivers would be calculated using the following formula:

$$Driver\ A\ Score \quad = \quad \frac{Driver\ A\ Actual\ Performance\ -\ Threshold\ *}{Driver\ A\ Target\ Performance\ -\ Threshold}$$

*Threshold is the lowest tolerable level of performance

Figure 7.7   NationJet's Value Weighting

Value Driver Category	Weight	Specific Value Drivers	Weight
Individual performance targets	50%	Driver A	50%
		Driver B	40%
		Driver C	10%
			100%
Team performance targets	40%	Driver D	60%
		Driver E	20%
		Driver F	20%
			100%
Business unit performance targets	10%	Driver G	50%
		Driver H	30%
		Driver I	20%
	100%		100%

NationJet's value-based compensation team developed the following example to illustrate how the incentive compensation would work. They started by looking at value driver performance. The following calculation shows the score for one of the value drivers.

Agent's Service Satisfaction Rating

$$= \frac{Driver\ A\ Actual\ Performance\ -\ Threshold\ *}{Driver\ A\ Target\ Performance\ -\ Threshold}$$

$$= \frac{8.9\ -\ 7.9}{8.6\ -\ 7.9}$$

$$=\quad 1.43$$

*Threshold is the lowest tolerable level of performance.

The agent's service satisfaction rating is combined with other agent specific drivers, as well as team and business unit drivers to complete the value driver performance table. Value driver category weights are applied to the value driver performance table to yield the overall value driver performance (see Figure 7.8).

The overall value driver performance is multiplied by the value driver bonus target to determine the value driver portion of the bonus. The business performance portion of the bonus is calculated in the same way as the value driver portion. The value driver performance was above targets in this example. As a result, the value driver portion of the bonus was also above target. Customer satisfaction is up, the employee's bonuses are up and, if the value model has correctly measured the value drivers, then shareholder value will be up as well.

Value Driver Bonus = Value Driver Bonus Target x Value Driver Performance

$$=\quad \$4,500\ x\ 1.18$$

$$=\quad \$5,310$$

NationJet's value-based compensation team wanted to ensure that the incentive compensation plan they develop encourages a longer-term perspective.

Figure 7.8   NationJet's Value Driver Score Results

Value Drivers	Weights	Performance	Score
Individual performance targets			
Agent's service satisfaction rating	50%	1.43	.72
Team player rating	40%	1.05	.42
Ticket accuracy rating	10%	.97	.10
			1.24
Team performance targets			
Team's service satisfaction rating	60%	1.21	.73
Average queue time	20%	.94	.19
Telemarketing script quality	20%	1.07	.21
			1.13
Business unit performance targets			
Res. ctr's service satisfaction rating	50%	1.24	.62
Cost per reservation	30%	.96	.29
Days advance ticketing	20%	.98	.20
			1.11
Overall performance targets			
Individual performance targets	50%	1.24	.62
Team performance targets	40%	1.13	.45
Division performance targets	10%	1.11	.11
	100%		1.18

They did not want the agents to take action that will benefit their yearly bonus at the expense of NationJet's future. They brought a longer-term perspective to the plan through a bonus bank. The team proposed that agents' annual bonuses be deposited in the bonus bank, and annual withdrawals would equal one-third of the balance. Figure 7.9 shows an example of how the bonus bank would work.

The bonus bank also makes it possible to declare a negative bonus. The example shows a beginning-of-the-year balance, how much bonus is earned throughout the year, and what is earned in consecutive years. Note that in 1999 there is a negative bonus, which illustrates the varying amount of payouts. There is clearly much greater stability to bonuses paid versus bonuses earned. Employees can have a negative bonus year but still collect under the bonus bank

Figure 7.9   NationJet's Bonus Bank Program

	1997	1998	1999	2000	2001	2002
Beginning of the year balance	0	4,940	9,287	5,664	7,456	11,518
Bonus earned for the year	7,410	8,990	-790	5,520	9,820	8,990
Bonus bank balance before bonus payment	7,410	13,930	8,497	11,184	17,276	20,508
Bonus paid (1/3 bank balance)	$2,470	$4,643	$2,832	$3,728	$5,769	$6,836

concept. The negative year, of course, affects the long term, but by using the bonus bank, averaging is employed, thus reducing the year-to-year fluctuations.

With the bonus bank, consecutive years of poor performance translate into a negative balance for the person's bank. While the employee is not held responsible for the deficit, the negative balance would become a very real incentive for the employee to leave the company because even in good years, earned bonuses would only serve to help decrease the deficit in their bank. They could see that they had dug a hole that wasn't worth climbing out of. The fact that future bonuses are tangibly jeopardized by poor performance years is usually a compelling reason for poor performers to leave the company. In standard compensation programs that do not feature bonus banks, each year is a clean slate, so not making bonus is less painful, making it harder to compel underachievers to leave. The NationJet compensation team thinks that it is appropriate that agents who cannot contribute toward NationJet's value, should be discouraged from remaining with the company.

Changes to Company Infrastructure

All this requires changes to a company's infrastructure. The existing performance system is an extremely important part of an organization. Very often, how people are compensated in a company is a tradition fraught with long-held procedures that simply cannot be changed overnight. The corporate culture will always impose constraints. For this reason, the strategy employed when introducing value-based compensation is to link it to existing infrastructure as much as possible, always aware that new concepts must be nurtured and supported to reap their full benefits. This begins with a performance-measurement system that is of high integrity. When people can believe the numbers on which company performance is based, it brings a new validity and integrity to all compensation at every level.

Integrity of the numbers begins with the identification of value drivers which is determined through value modeling. Value drivers form the basis for value-based performance measures. To further the integrity of a system, a company should use valid performance benchmarks to set performance targets by testing the benchmarks in its value model. Next, a mechanism should be created to resolve any inconsistencies between value-driver performance and overall performance. As has been mentioned many times, the value model reflects the best understanding of a business, so it only makes sense that the value model and value-based compensation programs be adjusted to resolve any misalignment between value-driver performance and overall business performance. Finally, initial training and ongoing support is critical to create and nurture an understanding of value-based compensation and associated performance measures.

In one extreme, some skeptics might suggest that value-based compensation should not be introduced until there is a working understanding in an organization of value-based ideals. In a perfect world that would be the perfect approach. But in reality, balancing the move toward value-based compensation with an organization's move toward value-based management is the best course. It is never too early to begin helping people understand how they individually affect value in their company, and there is nothing to lose by motivating them to do so early in the process. During modeling, identifying value drivers and conducting sensitivity analysis gives people a wider grasp of value-based concepts. Their depth of acceptance for value-based incentive programs will increase proportionately, ultimately giving way to a compensation program that will reap significant rewards for all concerned.

Chapter 8

VALUE-BASED PLANNING
Planning to Respond to Constant Change

If George Braga, the CEO at NationJet, has made any errors so far, they have been in the area of corporate planning, which he allowed to continue as it had in the past. The process had been started before he joined the company and he had too many other issues to address. When he asked his head of planning to describe the process to date and to give him an overview of the draft plans, he had a terrible sinking feeling. When the draft plans submitted by the business units were value tested by the planning group, Braga learned that the three-year business plans would destroy value for his company. In fact, as illustrated in Figure 8.1, only the reservations group was producing a return above the cost of capital and it was planning to shrink its asset growth.

To make it worse, Braga discovers that the effort of just getting to this point had been enormous. The strategic planning began the previous January, with a "visioning" session. Like programs at other companies, NationJet's visioning day took place in a picturesque country inn, a pleasant retreat far removed from the bustle and distraction of everyday events at head office. It was intended to give management the opportunity to separate themselves from the daily grind, relax and think creatively. It was interesting and fun to have senior managers and executives together. At the time, Braga's only regret had been that the sales managers had not been present to describe what they were seeing in the marketplace.

The group reconvened in April to consider planning guidelines, which were distributed to everyone who would participate in planning. A series of

Figure 8.1   NationJet — Value of Business Plans

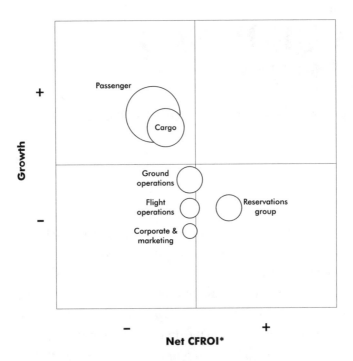

* Cash Flow Return on Investment

planning meetings were held in late May and early June. The guidelines contained all the standard tools and forms—Strengths, Weaknesses, Opportunities and Threats (SWOT) analysis, growth-share matrix, five-forces analysis and so on. The planning department provided an orientation session on planning for the team. An analyst explained each of the planning tools and the participants found the process interesting. But the most instructive discussions occurred during breaks and at lunch, and somehow these didn't fit into the forms used for strategic planning. Braga couldn't help but feel that something was lost because of that.

Later that summer, reports and templates for the preparation of the three-year financial projections associated with the strategic plan were distributed. Many people worked long hours throughout September crunching the numbers for the budget. In mid-October, the budgets were aggregated and reviewed. The plans were then analyzed for value before presentation to Braga.

The CEO now realized he had made a big mistake in letting the process drag on so long. The plans and budgets lacked ambition. The head of planning said that he had sent back initial plans because excessive conservatism was obvious. Challenged to improve their figures, managers responded in a variety of ways. Some increased their revenue targets, or lowered expenses. Others focused on defending their initial budgets, recognizing that their perceived success in the company and their incentive compensation would be linked to actual performance versus budget.

But projected net income in the budget's first year was still less than the company would earn in the current year and two major units were destroying value. Braga now realized that months of work to produce a strategic plan that his team had sincerely believed would grow the firm, had been a complete waste. How could this have been avoided?

It is indeed possible to avoid the many frustrations and failures associated with strategic planning. And frustrate they do: a survey in the mid-1980s of multibusiness firms by researcher James Brian Quinn found that while companies surveyed remained firmly committed to strategic planning, a startling 87 percent reported disappointment and frustration with their systems. The NationJet CEO, is not alone. But where do the problems reside?

Almost every company spends a huge effort on planning but ends up dissatisfied with the result. Typically the process results in plans that say one of two things: everything is just great and we will achieve a percentage increase over last year, or that things are tough now but it will get fixed in the last year of the plan. That is not good enough. It is overly formal, does not provide for anything that is a breakout strategy and does not allow for responsiveness to new opportunities. Why then does this continue? Because the planning process is so institutionalized and drives so much of the historical results-based management process that people are reluctant to change.

Planning forms the social contract between the levels in the organization and is the traditional basis for assessing ongoing performance. Accordingly, if the value enterprise is to become a reality, value must be fully integrated into this process. This may in fact be one of the biggest challenges on the Value Journey. Fortunately, there are important and practical solutions.

George Braga decided to take matters into his own hands. He met with managers several times to review the budgets and make changes. He informed them of these high-level changes and asked them to integrate the figures into their plans. He explained that to get capital for expansion they would have to show how they were going to produce returns above the cost of their capital. The managers were frustrated by all this but they held group sessions to identify how they would meet this new criterion. They spent most of December crunching numbers to come up with a budget that complied with the changes Braga imposed. Frustration was high because they had business units to run and wanted to be done with a planning process that seemed to go on forever. There was no time to evaluate reports of changing customer preferences or to reflect on the acquisition of a commuter airline by Budget Airways, their major competitor, the previous September. Braga sensed his managers' frustration. He treated them to a special Christmas staff dinner at which he expressed his appreciation for all their efforts.

By the first week in January, one year after the process had started, Braga had reassessed the plans. He concluded that they were not as good as he would have liked and there was no point in going further. What was he going to do? His people were exhausted from planning and the company couldn't continue delaying action on many of the significant challenges that had emerged in the marketplace during that time, changes that weren't addressed in the strategic plan. Braga knew that the old process was fundamentally flawed and had to be replaced.

Clearly, institutional strategic planning was a failure, out of touch with the realities of NationJet's real-world activities. Researcher Quinn found that, "formal planning systems rarely formulated a corporation's central strategy. The annual planning process itself was rarely [if ever in the study] the source of new key issues or radical departures into entirely different product/market realms." [1] A study by Walter Kiechel was even more damning. It found that fewer than 10 percent of corporate plans are successfully implemented.[2]

The Failure of Traditional Strategic Planning

What's the underlying problem with strategic planning? In his book *The Rise and Fall of Strategic Planning*, McGill University professor of management, Henry Mintzberg, asserts that the traditional process that companies like NationJet use is bankrupt. A structured, calendar-driven approach to planning cannot foster the elements that create true strategy: informal learning, creativity and flexibility. He argues that the process must be reconceived to emphasize informal learning, personal vision and real time analysis.

Serious change in a corporate strategy tends to be associated with discontinuity, and things that don't have patterns, trends or known states. In the 1970s, the Arab oil embargo turned the oil and gas industry, and much of the economy, upside down. Strategic planning could not predict it, yet it had such an impact that the industry was fundamentally redefined. Strategic change almost always comes as a result of the very things that planning is least able to handle – unexpected change.

Strategy formation often loses touch with operations management. Mintzberg identifies a distinction between the "formulation of strategy, a task restricted to the important people in the organization [...] and the implementation of strategy, the job of everyone else."[3] Senior executives usually conduct the planning analysis that leads to the direction strategic planning will take among themselves, divorced from the day-to-day realities of line managers. The company then faces the problem of how to link newly created general strategy objectives to specific real-life operations. Detachment also affects budgeting, which is an operational expression of strategy. Budgets rarely express the lofty ideals of strategic planning; too often they are merely reflections of achievable goals to secure management bonuses. Because managers don't want to fail they negotiate easily met goals. They do not have an interest in coming up with stretch strategies that may require extraordinary things from them. Only incremental change results, despite a constantly changing environment.

So if formal planning is ill conceived and really the wrong approach to create innovative, far-reaching strategy for business, why do organizations continue to use it? Just as custom and habit cemented the use of traditional accounting practices, the same can be said about formal planning. While it hasn't been around as long as accounting, the tendency for an organization is to cling to existing processes and things that it knows. This is age-old. James Brian Quinn offers this explanation for the persistence of traditional planning, "It provided a mechanism through which earlier strategic decisions were confirmed. In other words, planning helped to codify as well as formalize agreed-upon goals and commitment patterns. In the decision-making sphere, it provided a systematic means for evaluating and fine-tuning annual budgets."[4]

While the process may be seriously flawed it cannot be completely scrapped. NationJet, and other companies suffering from planning paralysis, should adopt value-based planning, an informed, comprehensive process.

How does a company build a new framework that will foster the informal learning, creative environment, and real-time reaction to day-to-day events that are so critical to effective value-based planning? A recent article in *BusinessWeek*[5] noted that after taking a backseat to other concerns in the 1980s, strategic planning is back in business "with a vengeance." But only organizations that practice strategic planning with a difference enjoy positive results. The difference is the absence of the abstraction, the top-down hierarchy, and the isolation from the day-to-day operating realities of businesses. The new approach democratizes planning by, "handing strategic planning over to teams of line and staff managers from different disciplines. Frequently, these include junior staffers, handpicked for their ability to think creatively, and near-retirement old-timers willing to tell it like it is."[6] It also includes significant interaction with key customers and suppliers.

Gary Hamel, a guru of the new strategy, describes the process in even broader terms. He argues that in addition to democratizing the process, strategy formation in companies should be about changing rules and even creating tomorrow's industries. He asserts that strategic planning should be an opportunity to pull out all the stops; to "change the rules of an industry to its advantage,"[7] just as Wal-Mart did in discount retailing or Charles Schwab did in the brokerage and mutual fund business. The notion that strategic thinking and its resulting changes might only be incremental is unacceptable to Hamel and other advocates of a democratized strategy process. He says: "It's imagination, not resources, that is scarce. So we have to involve hundreds if not thousands of new voices in the strategy process if we want to increase the odds of seeing the future." [8]

J.M. Smucker, a US company that makes jams and jellies, recently opened its strategic planning to a much broader range of players. The company enlisted 140 employees, 7 percent of its workforce. For six months the group devoted almost half of its work time to a major strategy exercise. "Instead of having just 12 minds working it we really used the team of 140 as ambassadors to solicit input from all 2,000 employees," said President Richard K. Smucker. "It gave us a broader perspective, and it brought to the surface a lot of people with special talents."[9] A company in a slow-growing, mature market, Smucker's emerged from the innovative strategy process with no fewer than a dozen viable new initiatives that probably will double its revenues over the next five years. One of the more exciting ideas was an alliance with a candy company to make Smucker's jellybeans. The idea came from a team of employees that ordinarily would not have had a role in the strategy process.

By inviting a broader range of people to the strategy table, Smucker's clearly increased their odds of accurately targeting the future. As *BusinessWeek* observes, many companies are deciding that it is worth taking risks to get the strategy process right. When companies get their strategies wrong, the results can be disastrous in a remarkably short period of time.

Getting strategic planning right primarily means assuring people that ideas will be solicited at every level of the organization, and then executed in a timely way. Democratizing planning and carrying it out expeditiously in the context of the strategic vision are central to successful business today. Every day, it is becoming more common for excellent companies to trade off a degree of accuracy for speed in everything they do. It's more important to mobilize for immediate action when events present themselves, than it is to make sure the situation fits into the preordained plan or budget. Waiting for the company's scheduled strategy session in April to discuss definitive industry events that took place in January, clearly puts a company at risk in a world where changes happen with lightning speed. A company shackled by a calendar-driven, top-down strategy will always be outperformed by competitors who, other things being equal, formulate strategy in real time and close to their operation.

Another problem surfaces. How can a company make sense of perhaps hundreds of ideas? How can the truly winning initiatives be separated from value destroyers in a timely way? Once again, the answer lies in the versatility of the value model, the mechanism that primarily defines value-based planning. The first thing value-based planning calls for is to focus strategic thinking on a company's value levers and value risks, the things that affect value. These, of course, were determined in modeling. By focusing a company's thinking on the real value drivers of the business, the strategy process is more likely to generate sound and executable ideas. Conversely, by knowing what the value risks are, the company can also direct its thinking about strategies to mitigate the consequences of an adverse turn of events. The value model, along with an assessment of strategic fit, becomes absolutely critical in making sense of the numerous ideas that will be generated through a more open, democratized process of planning. The model can help you assess each idea accurately for its value-creating potential. (There is another important aspect, that of a sound value infrastructure, which will be discussed in Chapter Nine.)

An excellent illustration of how critical the model is to assessing strategic ideas, came from a major electric utility. There was a tremendous void at this company between the engineers running the utility's generating facilities, the operating division of the company and the finance operation. Historically, whenever the engineers came up with ideas for new initiatives, as they did frequently because they were closest to the operating function, they had to submit them to finance for approval. The evaluation process was long and slow, generally taking up to four months.

The engineers always seemed to have good ideas of how to improve things technically but they were handicapped by the fact that they had a limited sense of which of their many proposals would create or destroy value. Their ideas carried multiple impacts company-wide. It simply wasn't possible for one engineer to know all the effects his initiative might have in other operating divisions. If something made sense in his sphere of influence, then from his perspective, it made sense to recommend it. For their part, the finance group would give equal time to each initiative submitted, regardless of whether it destroyed value or created it. Because of this drain on time, finance could rarely evaluate more than two or three projects per generating facility each year. The engineers, however, usually had at least ten new initiatives they thought were viable. That didn't matter. They recognized that the finance department would not be able to evaluate all their ideas, so they were faced with blindly narrowing the field. And of course, it sometimes turned out that the two they chose to submit were value destroying or not strategically aligned.

Sometimes a generating facility would not get any projects approved for the year. The void created between the engineers and the finance operation was understandable, as was the frustration and loss of confidence at the generating facilities. Over a six-month period a value model was developed for each generating unit. Once the model was built and in place, it took only one month to go through all the projects that the divisions had proposed or wanted to submit. The value-creating proposals were, of course, clearly revealed in the model long before they were sent to finance. The world opened up for the engineers. By employing the value model for their operating division, they could accurately assess and understand which initiatives were viable.

And as for finance, they suddenly had little work to do assessing initiatives. Because everything had previously been revealed and checked out in the model before submission, finance's role became that of a guide and partner to operations instead of an adversary. Their role in the company was transformed. Rather than the lengthy two- to four-month process, finance's function became one of evaluating the assumptions of the initiative. But without first building the models, and then employing them at each operating level, the company had been perpetually missing scores of good ideas, and was allowing a real divisiveness between divisions to grow.

Using Scenario Analysis to Address Uncertainty

Even with models and sound value-based planning it is still difficult to know what the future holds for a company. In traditional strategic planning, forecasting is used to understand what will happen tomorrow. But this is ineffective because it simply predicts what might happen in a broad, unspecific way, using yesterday's numbers. Value-based planning prepares for what might happen to a company in the future through scenario analysis. After there is a sufficient understanding of a company's value levers and value risks through modeling, the next step in planning is for a company to engage in specific scenario analysis. It can best be described as a method that allows a company to deal with the uncertainty of the future by looking at how its strategy might survive in the world of a specific scenario.

To clarify, remember that a company's strategy is what the company is planning to do inside its own walls. A scenario is what will happen outside those walls. Watching a scenario unfold in the model shows how to assess what is going to happen outside. Scenario planning looks at a wide range of possibilities in the marketplace. It is designed to explore the plausible, not to determine the probable. Each credible event can be considered a scenario. And by running the scenarios, or events, one by one and in combinations, through the model and watching them unfold, a company can get an accurate profile of the impacts and plan accordingly. This helps to determine just how robust certain strategies are with regard to various scenarios or combinations. A good company strategy is one that is robust under different plausible events.

To illustrate the versatility of scenario analysis, look at the Shell Oil Company. In the early 1970s, Shell began using scenario analysis in planning to generate mind-stretching, global issues to get company divisions to see things in a larger context. One of the events they explored was an extreme increase in foreign oil prices which would result in a need to reduce US dependence on foreign oil. At the time, the scenario was just one of several under consideration, but within a few years it had become a reality. Because Shell had considered the events in advance and created a strategy for handling it, they were prepared. Of the seven major US oil companies, Shell was the only one not taken completely by surprise by the actions of the Organization of Petroleum Exporting Countries. At the time of the crisis, Shell's revenues ranked last of the seven major companies but within a decade they had climbed to second and have remained there. Today, scenario analysis is the cornerstone for company strategy making.

Aligning Resource Allocation with Enterprise Value

A decentralized approach to strategy means that the senior executive team must redefine its role. Its job should become one of facilitation of strategic planning rather than of control over it. Individual business units must always own the strategies because they will play the key role in their formation. The executive team's activities then become centered on guidance rather than governance, shifting from being deterministic and control-driven to supportive and enabling. Of course, there will always be times where there is a need for objectivity and clarity in making decisions of which individual business units may not be capable.

These cases would include the often difficult circumstances surrounding portfolio decisions such as allocating capital, selling off business units or simply shutting them down. While it might be obvious to shut down a business unit according to the numbers, at the operating level, there is usually rationalization, which clouds the obvious. Managers usually do their best to convince superiors that a rosier picture is just around the corner, that the division is just in a cyclical downturn. Because of constituency bias and simply being too close to the situation, it would be imprudent for business unit managers to make those decisions. A senior-level objectivity and full understanding of integration issues revealed in the model are required to make those kinds of value-based planning decisions. But the tenor of the decision must reflect the decentralized role strategic planning process. The executive team should never play the role of general, giving orders and governing. It should be a supportive, benevolent referee, reserving the right to step in when difficult decisions need clarity and provide the ultimate challenge to the value-creation potential of plans.

The second key role that the executive team plays in value-based planning is one of integrating and capitalizing on the full use of the model. In many companies, one of the biggest integration issues is transfer pricing. When purchases are made from one business unit to another, how will pricing be structured? From a value-based perspective, it is usually counterproductive to allow the business units to settle all the issues surrounding transfer pricing. For this reason it should be the executive team's domain to set up an artificial marketplace.

The value-based theory on transfer pricing is that within a company, these prices should play the same role that prices do in the economy, which is, to achieve optimal economic allocation of resources. There is a big challenge in establishing transfer prices. From a value perspective, price is not as critical as whether the overall scheme results in value-creation. In order to know if transfers are creating the right behavior, it is necessary to look at the value model again. If a company understands how different business units function together, it can model the relationships to structure transfer prices to ensure value-creating behavior. The executive team's supporting role is enabled by the value modeling information. The senior executives become a steward of the rich information available through modeling, by accessing it, and employing it to inform portfolio decisions, transfer pricing, and sometimes morale issues.

Attributes of Value-Based Planning

Just what does value-based planning look like? It is very different from traditional planning in most companies. It has a significant shift in style. But since it is so central to how businesses are managed and decisions are made, it is a critical element of the Value Journey. Some key attributes of a truly value-based process include:

- full integration of strategic, tactical and operational plans to ensure consistency in decision making
- a rolling, forward-looking process to ensure optimal allocation of resources
- integration of trade-offs between revenue costs and capital to provide an appropriate focus on value
- sharing of planning information that is integrated, easily accessible and provided in multiple views to facilitate decision making
- highlighting of performance exceptions for analysis of future impacts
- creation of accountability for achieving value targets throughout the firm
- an adaptable and creative process for responding to internal or external events

Without this vision, planning managers will slip back to managing their independent budgets without regard to their impacts of value.

Value-Based Planning in Action

The NationJet story demonstrates just how ineffective traditional strategic planning can be, especially when a company is faced with having to react quickly to defining events. The company had been so mired in annual budgeting, and so preoccupied with outlining its three-year strategy, that it barely noticed critical changes in its industry. First, was the problem of catering. Most of NationJet's rivals are outsourcing their catering. As George Braga looked to the business plan for the unit it was clear that it would need significant capital over the next three years if catering were to be viable. He then faced making the first of these investments. He began a simple discounted cash-flow analysis (DCF) and established unit prices required to provide a positive cash return of the invested capital. The prices were 40 percent higher than those in the unit's current business plan.

He then investigated prices for similar services from outside suppliers and found he could get lower unit costs than those in his DCF analysis. He felt confident that investing more capital in the catering business was not going to create value. He commissioned a team to look at options for spinning off catering and outsourcing the service. Not investing in catering would also provide capital to grow the profitable reservations business. Braga saw that the value approach to capital allocation was going to be an important element of planning at NationJet.

The second major change NationJet faced was industry consolidation. The airline was incapable of reacting with any real-time strategy to this change and missed the opportunity to purchase a small commuter airline that had been snapped up by a competitor, EastJet. Since Braga had recently hired a new head of performance management from EastJet, he asked him how his rival had been able to move so quickly. His new manager told him that EastJet was practicing value-based planning. Their information nucleus was its business model. As likely scenarios were run through the model, it offered a comprehensive understanding of its business, complete with trade-offs and outcomes at every level of operation. The model provided a motion picture of the company as opposed to a budgetary snapshot. Once EastJet updated its model with the appropriate information, it could deliver a current budget at virtually any time. It had a distinct advantage. It was spared the many weeks of annual budget preparation and negotiation that has become such a drain on energy and morale for NationJet. Managerial focus was where it should be, on day-to-day operation and constantly evolving outside events.

EastJet got the news of the possibility of acquiring the commuter airline on a Friday afternoon. It immediately triggered a sequence of events. Sheila Smith, the person responsible for environmental and competitive screening, was a member of a team dubbed "corporate intelligence," a group responsible for up-to-the-minute industry and competitor information. By Friday evening, corporate intelligence e-mailed a team of executives, managers and employees, detailing the news. They were informed that a brief was being prepared, and that it would be available Saturday night via e-mail. Smith's team also told the executives and managers to rendezvous at the company "war room" at 6 a.m. Monday for a comprehensive strategy session. Their secretaries and assistants were advised to clear the calendars for Monday and make any necessary travel arrangements.

The war room was a key component in EastJet's planning. By displaying current information about customers, markets, competitors, technologies and processes on computers, it enabled the company to react with a real-time strategy to any set of events. It can be likened to a corporate version of NASA's Mission Control. The room itself is equipped with numerous monitors which allow the business team to study any number of different scenarios and value models for the company, its business units or competitors, at any level of detail. The function of the war room is to house all the key information for formulating and implementing strategy in one place. Beyond initial modeling, impetus for a company to test and probe different scenarios through the business model is always either proactive or reactive. Just a week earlier, a team of EastJet executives, managers and employees had used the war room for a day of proactive value testing of new ideas for one of its business units.

With the potential acquisition and related events, the war room session was on a reactive footing. The goal was to examine comprehensively the acquisition and then probe, test and update accordingly with complete access to all the technological tools the company had. As with Mission Control, information in a corporate war room enables a business team to absorb crucial facts to build a logical position and then implement it.

Monday morning dawned with the team arriving at the war room having read and thought about corporate intelligence's weekend brief. The team immediately began to brainstorm about the significance of the potential acquisition and related events, and then to develop some possible scenarios as to how it might impact the company. One of the key elements they addressed in developing scenarios was customer and employee impacts. It became obvious that the differences in cultures would be a key issue if the acquisition were going to work. Also, they saw some immediate benefits from being able to offer some significant routes that their customers have been requesting. The team immediately understood the value-creating potential of the acquisition and began to think about how to respond. They spent the morning updating scenarios. They tested a variety of potential strategies for the combined company by running them through the business model, with the outcomes appearing on the monitors around the room.

Throughout, they called in essential operations managers and employees to contribute insights. Additionally, a planning technician and analyst were enlisted to ease the continuous flow of information that added to the team's understanding. The team continually developed scenarios all day then ran them through the model, with the outcomes shown on the monitors for everyone to study. The combination of the war room and the versatility of the company's business model had endowed EastJet with a highly responsive information system that the business team could mobilize and manipulate whenever necessary. By the time the team broke for dinner around 9 p.m., they had developed and studied a wide enough range of scenarios that they were able to narrow the possibilities and the impacts. They defined two strategies and a range of acquisition prices that made sense for the company.

But their work is not over. As the business team headed home for the evening, the strategies were given to the planning analyst and technician who worked through the night running each one against the many different scenarios. The planning technician tracked the outcomes and had them ready

when the team reported to the war room the next morning. By 6 a.m. a com-
plete financial analysis and a list of issues to resolve were ready for
discussion. The last 24 hours had produced significant information to help the
team develop a clear understanding of what the acquisition strategy should
look like. The team started again to create a negotiating position for discus-
sions with the target to be held that afternoon — days, and perhaps weeks,
before NationJet could prepare itself.

With the negotiating position in hand the company met the commuter
airline. Its executives were astounded that EastJet knew so much about them
and were impressed by its analysis of the enterprise value which would be
generated by their merger. The meeting was a complete success and the
acquisition plans moved forward. Planning group's role throughout the
process was one of support. It designed and maintained the war room, facil-
itated the creation of corporate intelligence, and provided the analyst and
technician during the strategy session. But most importantly, the CEO had
fostered full use and integration of the model. So when the company had to
react quickly to events, the use of the business model, war room and the
resulting information were natural.

Ultimately, the value enterprise proactively created its environment in
answer to the defining events that took place in its industry. Whatever the con-
sequences of the acquisition finally were, NationJet's George Braga realized
that he not only had to build a better planning process but an infrastructure to
implement strategy effectively. Like EastJet, he must have a highly responsive,
real-time information system to create options. Through the versatility of the
business model and scenario analysis, and the flexibility of the war room, the
company had to be able to take a disciplined, high-probability approach to
defining events, as opposed to a random one.

A real-time, open strategy needs a strong infrastructure to build on. While
the logic and practicality of open, reactive strategy-making appeals to many
companies, most have a very difficult time making the transition because
they lack the infrastructure to put it in place. Just as a tree must have a hearty,
healthy root system in order to bear the best fruit, an organization must have
a strong, defined value infrastructure to feed the magic of what the model can
do. We will examine how to put that in place in Chapter Nine.

Chapter 9

VALUE INFRASTRUCTURE
Gathering Relevant Information

Vincent Gordon, a NationJet marketing executive, had just made an incredible observation at the weekly meeting of the airline's executive council. He noted that during the previous six months NationJet's business customers were repeat fliers 67 percent of the time, while their main competitors' customers are only 52 and 40 percent respectively. Gordon proudly announced that the firm enjoyed greater customer loyalty. This was welcome news to his audience—they had suspected something, but had no hard figures to support their intuition. Gordon's colleagues looked at him, then each other in astonishment. Where did he get that information they asked? The answer was that Gordon had been busy conducting market research; he had commissioned a report and analyzed it himself. Although the information appeared sound, the methods and analysis were not. It had not been produced in a systematic fashion.

While Gordon's customer insights may have been unique to his company, his methods were far too common. Information is often siloed—not shared outside an individual's or a division's domain—and generated in a random fashion. This results in reports in areas such as plant efficiency, customer insights or sales force effectiveness that are less than helpful and even misleading. In order for information to be rich, right and challenged, it has to belong to the entire organization and be subject to the scrutiny in both the methods and the underlying assumptions. Rather than producing a unique study about customer loyalty, Gordon's data should have been available routinely as part of the company's information-gathering infrastructure.

To be a true value enterprise, a company has to routinely get, and share data in such a way that it provides a real opportunity for everyone in the company to have the same clarity that Gordon had. And as we saw in Chapter Eight, it's vital to be able to react to situations that change so rapidly they can make Monday's strategic plan look like an antique on Tuesday. To achieve this, a value infrastructure has to be built that gets the data needed and fosters flexibility. Many of the ideas in this book are based on the availability and use of a rich set of information about the company, its competition and the environment. However, the ability to gather this information in the form required may be one of the biggest stumbling blocks to reaching the goal of the value enterprise. In many respects it is not because the data does not exist but rather, because there is no effective way to harness it and apply it to key decisions.

What is a Value Infrastructure

A value infrastructure is a vehicle for guiding the collection and analysis of information. It allows a company to have a systematic way of grooming information into a malleable format that can then be plugged into the decision-making framework. Information is the biggest impediment to an effective infrastructure. Companies often complain that their data prove incomplete or too inconclusive to base anything on. But data will never be complete. Collection and analysis is an ongoing process. The ability to make the leap from incomplete data to final decision is called managerial judgment, which must always be value based. An organization can't expect the value infrastructure and value programs to flourish without a decision-making process aligned with them.

It is an overwhelming task to rebuild a company's data infrastructure; however, a value framework that includes modeling makes the task manageable. Through models, the value framework becomes a guide for data collection and also a test for its relevance, allowing a company to collect and distill far less information, with much more clarity. In fact, most organizations collect far more data than they can possibly use, and don't even understand *why* they're collecting it. Sometimes they collect it "just in case." Value modeling allows them to understand which data are required.

Data is all about clarity. The more tangible and concrete the information, regardless of the context, the less political and abstract things become. Still, people can observe data and interpret them differently. But if the data are absent, people operate from their own view of the world and only look for, or mine, information that supports what they want to believe. In Vince Gordon's case, it was a preoccupation with promoting his work in developing customer loyalty. Like Gordon's case, these endeavors are usually well meaning. Who could argue with efforts at building customer loyalty? In many organizations, the fashion of uncoordinated data gathering means that the sum total of these efforts has diminishing or negative returns. While some data will need to be restricted owing to confidentiality, a company's overall goal should be to create an open environment where all employees can comprehend the business's numbers so they can understand how the organization works together. That puts an end to information fiefdoms.

Too many companies are data rich and information poor because they suffer from too much random data collection rooted in the bias of individuals like Gordon. So companies end up being guided by individuals with ad hoc data for support. This is particularly problematic when an organization tries to introduce new initiatives. Over time, many people in an organization tend to add to the data infrastructure but rarely if ever, reduce it. One-off studies will suggest a whole new data gathering requirement to support a new initiative without replacing anything in the old. These organizations build data junk piles, that need sifting in the future without anyone challenging what the new data should be replacing. The excuses for not making business decisions also pile up as we wait for the data to prove our point.

So how does a company distinguish between faulty and relevant data? Rely on the integrity of the organization's value models. The linkages they reveal will help decide what information is truly universal and needed to build a legitimate infrastructure. The models also identify critical data that is worth collecting with increased accuracy. It guides both what is needed and what is essential to best manage for value. Modeling forces everyone to understand all the pieces of their company and reveals the critical linkages, as well as any gaps in information. These gaps tend to be causal ones: data that connects two discrete pieces of information. In Chapter Six we discussed NationJet's food. Meal quality was going down and that was probably going to spark passenger complaints. But NationJet had an information gap: how many customers were estranged by the airline's decision to scrimp on food often got ignored in favor of customer feedback forms in seat pockets, a small sampling. More important to the airline was how many people actually complained about meal quality and how many of them were sufficiently exasperated that they took their business elsewhere?

In other cases, there can be stale data that is relied on year after year. NationJet's 1991 customer satisfaction survey on price sensitivity found that 30 percent of respondents were price sensitive. But what does that say about passengers in 1997? And are there differences between economy- and business-class customers that did not exist back then? The senior executive's role becomes one of articulating these things to the appropriate areas of the organization, enabling managers to truly refocus from making decisions based on intuition to those based on fact. To do this, an effective value infrastructure must be developed to produce a framework that supports real-time planning, creativity and the recognition of unexpected events.

Value Infrastructure Elements

The most daunting task for any executive developing and implementing a value program centers on how to address the implementation of infrastructure change. We have many clients for whom this process is overwhelming. Other clients require only an adjustment to their existing infrastructure. The key infrastructure elements that most commonly require consideration for an organization undertaking a value program can be divided into three major categories: People, Process and Technology.

1. People

    a. People Value Management

    b. Continuous Organizational Learning and Training

    c. Communications

    d. Center of Excellence

    e. Salary Surveys

2. Process

    a. Customer Value Management

    b. Modeling

    c. Reengineering the Reporting and Analysis Function

    d. Reengineering the Planning Process

3. Tools and Technology

    a. Enterprise-Wide Financial Systems

    b. Activity-Based Cost Management

    c. Benchmarking and Best Practices

    d. Data Warehousing

    e. War Room

PEOPLE

PEOPLE VALUE MANAGEMENT

The one sustainable resource that every business has is people, and they are the centerpiece of an effective infrastructure. But implementing an effective people infrastructure can be one of the more difficult challenges. Because it calls for some nontraditional data, its capture and construction are often inhibited by the traditional "activity spirals" that employees are caught in. Many companies are too busy to capture data on the activities of its own management. They lose touch with where management should focus its efforts in supporting overall strategy and key initiatives. In our consulting we often see organizations where managers talk about growth strategy but when asked where they spend their time, 80 percent say they spend it responding to cost-cutting and budget pressures.

These are two key areas where people infrastructure is crucial:

1. The exercise of capturing information related to how people in the company create value.

2. A clear understanding of the company's employee value in their jobs.

Documenting people data involves acquiring information to understand how employees create value. This is not limited to traditional head counts, training and compensation, but involves a comprehensive understanding of people and their activities at every level. The purpose is to understand which activities drive company value, by delivering benefits to customers or other employees.

A clear understanding of the value a company creates for its employees is critical. Many firms have something like this in place, known as pulse reports, voice of the employee or employee satisfaction. Few companies dispute the correlation between knowledge of how workers create value for customers and increased customer satisfaction. The same is true of a company's understanding of how it creates employee value: how much fulfillment and professional development does the company create for its workers? It recognizes the employee's right to evaluate the company's job and benefit offering versus the competitors'.

What does the organization do in material and nonmaterial terms to increase value for its employees? Is the company effectively addressing issues of balancing employees' working and private lives? Do they have overall confidence in your firm? What are their professional challenges? Companies often make use of employee satisfaction surveys, but these tend to be superficial and random. Knowing an employee's satisfaction does not tell you how to keep them. The information you need is broader and more comprehensive. It identifies and measures job quality attributes throughout the organization and also undertakes to identify patterns in employee turnover.

Almost all organizations take pride in describing people as their "most valuable asset" but very few take inventory of it. They keep records of their other assets—financial and physical plant—but they spend no time understanding people. A good method is to build a balance sheet of the skills and competencies that now exist in the organization as well as those gained from new employees or lost to attrition. The company will then see whether it's improving its capability of meeting employee needs and creating value for them, or whether it is simply replenishing itself with employees. Companies need to match skills and competencies with the company's future strategy for people. Building a balance sheet of employee assets quantifies this. It would keep the corporation's blood fresh, its thinking youthful. It would also enable an employer to increase employee competencies over time to match its overall strategy and the evolving value-creating opportunities. As the organization matures and its relationship with your customers evolves, it will need to develop significantly different growth oriented competencies.

Skandia Foersaekrings AB, based in Stockholm, is doing precisely this. Recently they added an entire section of their annual report called "people asset" and they have a people measurement they call "return on knowledge." As a financial company where the principal resource is employee intelligence, it clearly puts great importance on measuring how effectively it learns, and how successfully it leverages people.

In most industries, retaining employees has significant long-term benefits. When employees remain at one company, they have a better idea of how to service customers and how to mentor new people in the organization. Although it may cost more to retain veteran employees, productivity normally rises with tenure. To understand the economics of employee retention, you must capture the appropriate data. Start with length of employment, then carefully track information by department, recruiter, skills and competencies. World-class organizations meticulously monitor these things and they invest in recruiting and retaining employees. They capture data from the employee's first day at the organization to their last, including exit interviews, to look for patterns that may reveal when recruiters or mentors have a higher than usual turnover, or a better than average result at developing leaders. This can be challenging because employees tend to move from one position to another often. But it is for this reason that data should be collected. Unfortunately, most organizations generally choose to ignore the patterns that surround employee retention or worse, rationalize them away.

Getting this information begins with focus groups and employee value surveys to identify and measure job quality attributes. Commission job quality and compensation surveys of your industry as well as within relevant functional areas of your company to determine prevailing compensation. This is not a one-time effort, but a routine that must be established to deal with areas of growing demand. For example, in the past five years, so many companies have invested in important software applications that there is a huge demand for technicians to implement them. Their salaries have soared. Many companies weren't even aware that software technicians for their in-house applications were in such demand, and were underpaying them. As a result they begin resigning, wooed away by other companies with better compensation. In this way, organizations lost an important group of employees. Remember that most employees do evaluate their jobs compared to other organizations. Many companies are up to the minute on capital and commercial markets, which are shareholder and customer focused, but have little understanding of individual labor markets. But their employees do, and this includes not only salary but also the entire compensation package, such as benefits, health and holidays. Unfortunately, few companies consider them important. The prospect of capturing employee data is daunting but the information is accessible, manageable and because of its relevance, warrants the effort. Once that information has been gathered, a model of employee value should be built incorporating everything found in employee focus groups and surveys, and these linked to the overall value model of the company.

CONTINUOUS ORGANIZATIONAL LEARNING AND TRAINING

We had a client who linked cash measures and growth with the compensation program for all employees. It actually saw unplanned and significant growth in the organization, and the new cash measure began to diverge from the net income that they had traditionally been paid on. So the employees thought their performance was improving but the cash measure was actually showing that they were heading in the opposite direction. Analysis indicated that growth required an investment in the organization, so the cash measure would actually go down. But employees wrote angry letters referring to the stupid performance measures, that there really was no link between their performance and cash flow, that the human resources department did not understand what direction the company should take, and that they were delivering the growth the company had asked for but being penalized for it. Amazingly, the human resources director said that training would probably solve the problem. It was amazing, because the year before, when the company had instituted the measure, they had decided not to train because it would be too expensive. They decided that employees would figure out the scheme on their own over time.

Although Peter Senge's *The Fifth Discipline: The Art and Practice of the Learning Organization*[1] sold 400,000 copies, very few organizations have fully grasped the steps necessary to bring this ambitious endeavor into reality. It's far too common. Everyone in the organization has to be trained on what value creation is all about. To develop value-based competencies, the commitment to learning and training must be unwavering. Learning never ends. It must begin at the executive level where performance reviews and operational discussions include the hard questions related to value trade-offs. The next step is teaching the language of value. Management must reinforce and nurture this language every day. When the opportunity to link training to everyday life is missing, learning goes into cold storage and is only brought out again with great pain. Companies often have to retrain under less than ideal conditions when there is an emergency or an unexpected opportunity requires quick action.

Training must reflect how employee, customer and shareholder value are inextricably linked on a day-to-day basis. It must balance both quantitative value mechanics and the qualitative management. It must ease the development of value language. Throughout the process, it will be very tempting to revert to traditional methods, measures and language, especially during budgeting and performance reviews. Good approaches include internal communication vehicles such as newsletters, bulletins, and intranet sites, with discussions on value-creation results, to remind people consistently of the value transformation taking place.

Value-based management merges the disciplines of operations, strategy and finance. While most managers have a good understanding of one area, and perhaps some are conversant in two, few are expert in all three. Thus the need for comprehensive cross-functional training. Training must be specific and tailored, not simply off-the-shelf programs. Teach employees which specific value drivers they affect and therefore which specific performance measures they should manage. They must know how their areas of responsibility link with the rest of the business. The center of excellence, as discussed in the next chapter, will play a critical role. The other area of significant training will be related to value modeling. Those people responsible for building and maintaining value models must become conversant with dynamic system modeling tools and techniques so they can grow into a key role of teaching the organization.

Throughout training, it is essential to match training tools to people's aptitudes. To allow people to feel comfortable and not embarrassed by what they don't know, we strive to use computer tools that are not excessively complex. For example, we use the following training modules in teaching value-based principles:

- Basics of finance
- Time value of money
- Value-based management concepts and principles
- Advanced topics in value-based management
- Value-based management tools and techniques
- Role of capital in value creation

Without training, employees will never fully grasp the sense of value-creation throughout the company. This is wasteful and counterproductive. Even worse would be for them to learn about it in a piecemeal fashion, around the watercooler or through distorted rumors and hearsay. Establish a comprehensive, ongoing training approach to make the most of the investment in value creation.

COMMUNICATIONS

Internal and external communication must be consistent throughout. This is particularly important in large organizations with multiple newsletters, briefings, news releases and advertising. This involves first developing the key themes. These will serve as the building blocks for all communications. Then, communicating the message often, particularly inside the company. In many organizations with which we have worked, we have conducted a "change diagnostic" to assess progress of the value program implementation. A change diagnostic is a detailed employee survey to identify specific elements of resistance to change, the organizational or behavioral impediments to executing change with the enterprise. Often, the critical shortcoming cited by employees is not their understanding of the principles or the need to adopt this perspective, but the inconsistency of messages from senior management.

Another common technique which could be effective is the use of corporate intranets. This medium could be used to both make performance measures available to managers, and then determine if the information is being accessed by measuring the "hits" on each measure.

CENTER OF EXCELLENCE

A center of excellence requires people to provide the momentum for carrying out value programs. Participants are internal consultants who have experience with finance, operations and strategy, with capabilities to operate across all functional areas. They are teachers, architects, builders, judges and change agents who come from virtually every area of the company. (Some companies treat this as a job rotated among people, providing them with an important stepping stone for career development.) The center needs a team because seldom will all of the requisite skills reside in one or two people. Many organizations have similar units currently called performance groups. The team's goal is to be a partner with operations in value creation and for this reason, it should have multiple locations within strategic operating units. The center of excellence should be considered a prestigious position, and one that has some stringent criteria and high admission requirements. Because it is a nontraditional activity, it can sometimes be difficult to start. In the beginning, people may feel that it is just another ivory tower. This should not be the case. Because the center of excellence will be located at the operating level and will work intimately with it, its impact will be direct. Expect initial misgivings, so make a real effort to jump-start the concept and imbue it with sufficient momentum. Teach the organization about the center's requirements; show everyone how it will be sustained and give the mandate to cut across organizational boundaries. To make the center vital, operations must commit to it.

Tell them at the beginning that future center members will be drawn directly from operations. Implementation will ease a consistent, ongoing flow of value information throughout the company. Target performance levels should be established for the center. We often suggest that the center target ten times its annual budget in value creation opportunities per year.

SALARY SURVEYS

An important element in employee value infrastructure is the assessment of current market price for similar skill levels, effort and employee potential. The value enterprise will seek this information out proactively and react quickly instead of waiting until the market passes it by and critical people quit. There are several companies that publish salary surveys and related employee expense. It is important to recognize that these organizations seldom publish other comparisons of the "soft side" benefits that so often generate employee churn. Innovative techniques are required to get a holistic picture of your employee value in a competitive market. Finally, take care to ensure that appropriate normalization is done across geographical areas and industries. Pay scales in New York differ from those in Omaha. CFOs in telecommunications have different responsibilities from their counterparts in consumer products industries.

PROCESS

CUSTOMER VALUE MANAGEMENT

Customer value management is an important new process. Many companies now focus on the high costs of acquisition and retention of customers. They are scrambling to get a data infrastructure to do this, but the truly progressive ones are treating customer value as a process in itself. How you acquire a broader knowledge of customer value is similar to what you'll do for employee value. Unlike employee value, data on customers exist in droves. But most organizations don't have a systematic way of structurally getting the data into a usable form that can then be plugged into decision making. As with employees, customers are an asset to an organization. Track them with a balance sheet to understand their number and quality, as well as the ebb and flow of your relationship with them. The information must be documented from customers, as well as the entire marketplace, so that a company can understand the value proposition it creates for its customers relative to its competitors. It must be constantly on the lookout for marketplace signals that indicate a shift in the value proposition of its customer base. Tracking the information is the first step in assuring that the company focuses on it. This should be followed by the information of customer focus groups that will serve as a basis for segmenting customers and for creating customer surveys.

Telecommunications is one industry where understanding customers is critical. In that industry, there is frequent customer turnover, known as churn. Although there are huge amounts of data existing for understanding churn, telecoms typically focus on a net difference in the number of customers. The data usually track only the numbers of customers who come and go. But there is a tremendous amount of valuable data in assessing the quality of the lost customers and the quality of the acquired customers, based on their long-term value. It must take into account not only revenue but the cost to serve certain customer segments, the degree of complexity needed to serve those segments, the referral potential, the margin, the price and the probable time they will stay with the company. So this vast amount of customer data that was formerly viewed in only one way, can be the basis for some very enlightening information that could lead the company to new revenue paths. There's greater clarity in customer data about where a company should focus its efforts. This information would then be used to build a customer value model to link the overall value model of the company.

MODELING

To distinguish the value enterprise from the common data dump, the company should construct an information infrastructure driven by its value needs. Customer and employee satisfaction data must be coupled with operational process data within the organization to enable immediate, flexible decision making. Many decision tools exist which turn this data into information a decision maker can use. The problem becomes how can value-driven decisions be constructed and evaluated from such a complex and diverse collection of data turned into information.

A company's information architecture should be organized around developing modeling competency to create a unifying decision support framework. Modeling provides decision makers a flexible and robust platform for scenario analysis. It allows for the cost-benefit weighing of policies to improve customer and employee satisfaction. This can be accomplished from both a qualitative and quantitative perspective if information is gathered to meet the modeling information requirements.

Customer and employee analysis must be geared toward the constant creation of data on how satisfaction is perceived over time. This includes the examination of causes for customer and employee loss as well. The identification and tracking of customer perceptions from across all channels of interaction between the firm and the customer must be considered. Build permanent "Satisfaction Data Groups" to provide a central and timely resource for applicable customer and employee satisfaction. Paired with this data should be "Operational Data Groups" which gather operational measures. The measures would consist of hard (as opposed to perceived) quantities that can be captured from operations. Ideally these measures would be chosen as important indicators for customer satisfaction attributes, employee performance, as well as operational efficiency and effectiveness. Many of the measures this group would collect come from traditional decision tools such as data mining on data warehouses and enterprise-wide applications. A separate "Model Decision Group" would then draw on the two data areas and from managerial mental models to construct value decision tools. The modeling data requirements would provide directional focus for customer and employee satisfaction and operational measure gathering.

Tracking variations provides insight into which operational areas create satisfaction. With this, ways to set industry standards in customer and employee satisfaction and to improve shareholder value can be explored. A company's value models will help teach value concepts to its managers by helping them focus on how cash flow is generated and where it comes from. They can see the complex interaction of strategic decisions, resource allocations, and satisfaction. This provides employees with a tool for evaluating short- and long-term value trade-offs.

There are two avenues for developing competence in modeling. An organization must create data groups focused on gathering timely data on satisfaction and operational measures. Also, a central modeling group must integrate the available data and create value models that help with value decisions. Setting up dedicated groups for data collection isn't novel to most organizations, given the satisfaction and operational measure focus, although monitoring data quality will be a whole new issue. It's harder to form a modeling group. But they can call on available modeling tools, including spreadsheet software and dynamic modeling software to perform elaborate simulations. These tools help create and maintain elaborate model interrelationships.

Unfortunately, to model properly requires more than opening a new package of software—it demands synthesizing the company's complex relationships and linking them to the efforts to create stakeholder value. Because learning takes time and tools, many organizations we have worked with have purchased the tools and contracted out the modeling. They delegated key employees to work with the contractor to learn effective modeling. Remember, the tools are only tools, the real power is in the modeling process itself.

REENGINEERING THE REPORTING AND ANALYSIS FUNCTION

How often are finance departments referred to as bean counters? How often are they removed physically from the operating groups and seen to reside in an ivory tower? How often do they manage a company by numbers, rather than operational realities? Finance often gleans insight from numbers only to encounter resistance from business unit managers who claim that while finance's ideas sound great they don't understand how things work out in the field.

In a value enterprise, where operations, strategy and finance are integrated in a single framework, the finance organization tends to be the crossroads where all the disciplines meet. It defines linkages that make the implicit understanding of the business explicit. Competitive challenges require finance to broaden its perspective and take a proactive enterprise-wide role. To play this role, the finance function must be world class, which means becoming value-focused measurement experts, while at the same time managing assets, risks and transaction processing with a high degree of efficiency and effectiveness. This, of course, is an emerging effort in the beginning, with the ultimate goal being a new set of competencies and organizational responsibilities for finance.

A characteristic required of reporting and analysis is being value-focused, which means always managing the business to maximize enterprise value. It means excellence in performance measurement—developing critical gauges of value for the organization. Capital management must be aggressive, and link capital allocation to the creation of enterprise value while focusing on improving cash flow and working capital productivity. It demands comprehensive risk management, applying consistent principles to significant exposures by rigorously identifying financial risk, core business risk, operational risk and legal and regulatory risk. And it must have an effective and efficient infrastructure, which focuses the activities of the finance function on value.

In Chapter Four, we talked about the superiority of cash flow to traditional accounting, and how all systems in a value-based company must be able to track cash to optimize value-based management. Clearly, the finance department must know how to accomplish this, as well as how to teach managers basic cash-flow skills such as how to calculate after-tax operating cash flows, or how to link operational drivers to financial outcomes.

The finance organization plays two broad roles implementing value-based management as illustrated in Figure 9.1. The first is that finance be partners with business units in pursuing value-creating opportunities. Finance must work with managers to define linkages between operational drivers, customer value, and shareholder value. Secondly, it must also be the catalyst in realizing value for the company. The finance organization should take the lead by managing the company's dealings with capital markets and communicating with the investment industry in order to ensure that the value that the company creates is realized in the capital marketplace, while also recognizing that as they push these concepts, finance will have to demonstrate its own value-creating potential.

REENGINEERING THE PLANNING PROCESS

We stated in Chapter Eight that planning is the most challenging and demanding of everything described in this book because of its pervasiveness and

Figure 9.1   A Value Infrastructure Supports Both Value Creation and Value Realization

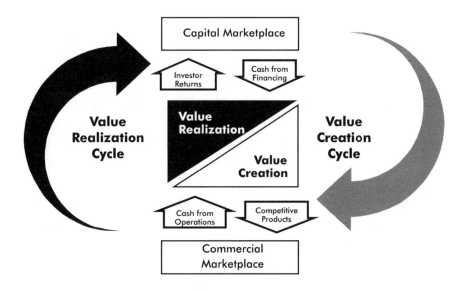

Financial Strategies
- Investor Relations
- Acquisitions/Joint Ventures/Spin-offs
- Monetize Non-productive Assets
- Refinancing
- Balance Sheet Restructuring

Operating Strategies
- Resource & Capital Allocation
- Product Pricing
- Process Reengineering
- Operational Restructuring
- Working Capital Management
- Productivity Improvement

complexity. A company may need one or two technical experts who are capable of integrating multiple dynamic value models from different parts of the business. Some organizations use workshops in lieu of seminars to encourage discussions, and these rigorous discussions help managers understand the trade-offs and insights.

The biggest challenge with planning and integration lies in managing the "white space" opportunities. These are potential areas of growth that often seem like blanks that can be ignored because they don't match the traditional skills of the existing business units, or they don't fall within the boundaries of the division. Managing white space is difficult because the real opportunities in most companies operate across boundaries. They are not confined and are not always obvious. It takes teamwork and a strong understanding of the integration of all the pieces. This brings us back to the reason modeling is so crucial to effective planning. It allows a company to gain holistic perspective of the enterprise so that it can manage the white space.

Because planning and models always focus on that great uncertainty—the future—scenarios need to be developed. They help to understand how attributes of customer-perceived quality will change over time, and what things probably trigger those changes. Situations need to be developed for how employee-perceived quality is likely to change and how sociological or other changes are likely to trigger this change. Think of environmental regulations demanding changes to engine design or car size. Or think of the oil shocks of the 1970s suddenly creating a demand for small autos. You need to develop scenarios for how competitors and partners could potentially evolve. For example, maybe your company has good partners now, but perhaps one of the vendors is not EDI-capable, so think about how to maintain the relationship. Perhaps Vendor B is a better choice because of its EDI status, even though you don't have as strong a personal relationship with them. A company has to develop the capabilities to engage in scenario planning effectively. In most cases it will mean using the industry's experts and futurists in general. This may mean contracting for outside services that can help create scenarios relevant to the business. When it comes to generating scenarios, knowledge is definitely power. Recognize that scenario analysis does not mean just looking at best and worse cases and taking the average, small-probability events with big impact must be understood. For further discussion of how to generate scenarios, read *The Art of the Long View* by Peter Swartz.

TOOLS AND TECHNOLOGY

ENTERPRISE-WIDE FINANCIAL SYSTEMS

Financial information technology is the cornerstone of the whole infrastructure. Most managers understand what data they need to make decisions, but are often bound by existing or legacy systems that prohibit them from capturing information systematically. We've talked about information "junk piles" that accumulate from overlaying more and more analysis. It's important to take that data, convert it into information and, ultimately, use it to support decisions. But while managers probably know what they already have, they can't find the data they want. So they commission a new one-time study that, while providing information conveniently, duplicates existing findings. This behavior is only a slight improvement over pure intuition. In many cases, finding the data to support a manager's intuition is no better than simply making decisions based on those hunches. Many companies spend big dollars on information-technology (IT) systems and data warehouses to tackle data piles. But despite the expense and fanfare, these new systems too often become the latest version of the data junk pile in the absence of a value-based decision framework. Rather than reshaping uncoordinated data, these systems should help a company build data collection, information, analysis and decisions. The goal is fact-based decisions.

To accomplish this, relevant data must be captured, both financially and operationally, for use in flexible ways. Since data will often be the biggest obstacle to value implementation, it is imperative that the data gaps be bridged. Inaccessibility of data in organizations that are tied to antiquated information systems has yielded a significant advantage to young companies. Many young, upstart companies not tied to inferior data-capture, but using state-of-the-art procedures, have had rapid and often phenomenal success in a variety of industries. The US long distance provider MCI successfully launched a product by manipulating its state-of-the-art (at the time) information technology. MCI's billing system was more flexible than its rivals and from that they could create a product, the well known "Friends and Family" program which has created some of the most loyal customers in the long-distance industry. MCI and other dynamic newcomers have faster, nimbler, more value-focused decision frameworks. Every company's data-capture system must be as technologically current as possible as well as being able to accommodate relevant information in many forms. It is particularly important to collect operational data. It ensures that the organization understands the drivers of transactions and activities and not just the financial outcomes associated with them.

ACTIVITY-BASED COST MANAGEMENT

Plenty of companies rigorously budget and examine the spending of capital. But there is unlikely to be a parallel process for how they allocate expense dollars on people and activities. Capital expenditure requires that the firm focus on the right markets, that the returns be adequate, that they earn above the cost of capital and that they have a positive net present value. Yet none of these procedures is required for the other 75 percent of the cost base. This is because there is insufficient data on what people do, or on the benefits of their doing it. Most company information systems have the ability to capture cost data. However, few accurately produce a granular analysis of the revenue and capital components needed to make an effective value assessment. Raw data must be converted into meaningful information. This includes multiple cuts of the same information to analyze value, for example, by customer, product, industry segment, sales team or geography. Flexibility to accommodate the rapidly changing competitive environment and its emerging value dynamics is vital to value-based management.

Activity-Based Costing (ABC), is a key element of the information infrastructure. ABC frameworks use flexible platforms to capture not only cost data, but revenue and capital at lower levels within the organization. In effect, ABC can model the costs as well as the benefits of a company's activities. Most organizations will have to significantly rework activity-based costing. ABC is flexible in obtaining "value activities" which may be the sum of several activities both within a process and across processes or organizational boundaries. Take, for example, the cost of customer acquisition, including sales, advertising and promotion. Imagine how worthwhile it would be if you knew the cost of acquiring new customers aside from the cost of keeping existing customers and what the impact of each is. ABC allows you to benchmark such critical processes to ferret out any value destruction deep inside your company and to refocus on creating value. You create value with future cash flows, not historical data. By using activities in lieu of costs, it is possible to forecast and plan for strategic value more appropriately.

It's common for organizations to reorganize continually and to create internal markets that include transfer prices in a bid to split up and deal with shared assets and shared benefits. They often lose sight of basic transactions. No amount of reorganizing sticks and boxes in organizations charts will preclude the basic definition of operations, which is: customers paying the company cash for goods or services. That does not change. So a company's understanding of cost and revenue data and shared assets and benefits must always return to this definition as the basis for organizing internal markets and transactions. World-class organizations often comfortably deal with shifts in products or reorganizations because they have a deep understanding of the data. They understand their basic processes and transactions in terms of volumes and costs, not just dollars, in the context of how they are creating value for the organization, its customers and employees. Which brings us back to the importance of aligning customer value with internal processes. Once a company understands its attributes of customer value, it can align its activities with the attributes to create informed decisions.

The service sector has grown significantly in recent decades. More and more of the activities in organizations today, are people driven, as opposed to machine driven. That means that people activities—be they customer or employee—must be fully grasped to help understand utilization of valuable assets and their cost and benefits. Just as business strove in the 1940s and 50s to understand machines and manufacturing, over time, with activity-based cost management, a company can gain the same understanding of its people and their activities. Activity-based cost management helps you do this by documenting not only just cost, but also the benefits, revenues and capital to support your company's activities.

BENCHMARKING AND BEST PRACTICES

The quest for performance improvement targets begins with the question, "Where does my company stand?" In sports, this question is easy since the rules of competition are well defined and the competition is easily understood. But in business this question quickly unravels into questions that are less clear. In what context? Relative to whom? Over what time? And stakeholder perspectives are not necessarily aligned. Customers, executive management, employees and shareholders have powerful and occasionally differing views about what constitutes effective corporate performance evaluation.

If management wants the business to improve continuously, it must measure results constantly and with best-in-class benchmarks. First, management must identify and rank those performance measures that directly drive cash flow and ultimately enterprise value. For certain financial elements these might include operating margins, market share, capacity utilization or inventory turnover. Next, it must determine from both its own historical performance as well its capital market peers the best-in-class targets in each of these areas for planning. Third, it must develop a clear map that relates allocation of capital and human resources to achieving these targets. And finally, it must measure actual results against the benchmarks and relate performance to actual value creation. For other customer, employee and process measures, you may have to resort to more elaborate techniques to ensure valid comparisons and set appropriate stretch targets. This often includes not only benchmarking numbers but evaluating the best practices and how the numbers are achieved. Once again, these benchmarks, if achieved, must create value for the organization—they need to be tested.

The key to any benchmarking lies in the methodology and the relevance of the information. Deloitte & Touche Consulting Group has established Peer*Scape* to help clients. Located on the Internet at www.peerscape.com, clients can access a continuous improvement methodology as well as a wealth of financial benchmarking information on more than 7,000 US-based companies. More than 45 performance measures over ten years are available for every company in relation to a selected peer group. These measures include shareholder value, financial and operational measures in an easy to understand graphic format. Companies can then link process-oriented results, such as order cycle times, to higher level performance measures to enhance continuous improvement.

DATA WAREHOUSING

It's a common story. After all the investment in hardware, software and networks much of the information needed by an organization is still inaccessible. Somewhere in the huge amounts of data available is the information needed, but there is no way of locating or consolidating it. This is where data warehousing comes into play. Corporate data typically exist in three levels—operations, informational and summary (see Figure 9.2). The data warehouse integrates, summarizes and provides information for managers and executives. It is used to support tactical and strategic decision making whereas operations data is used for day-to-day decision making. To support these needs, the data warehouse supplies different tools and levels of detail as required by each user.

Figure 9.2 Levels of Data

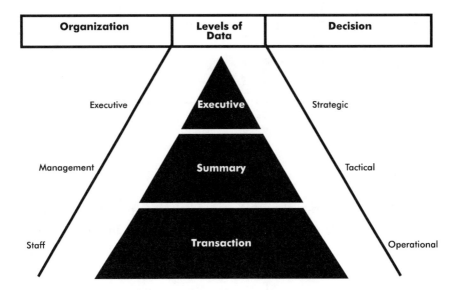

Business requirements exist within organizations at three levels. Each level requires the appropriate information and technology to enable decision making.

A data warehouse is technology (see Figure 9.3) that provides information collected from various operational systems. The information is often grouped into subject areas such as human resources and finance and stored in "time slices." Specialized databases store the large amounts of data and data analysis and reporting tools can provide users with access. Data mining tools allow users to determine hidden relationships, key attributes driving customer behaviors, and trends that might not otherwise be evident.

Figure 9.3   Data Warehouse Technology Environment

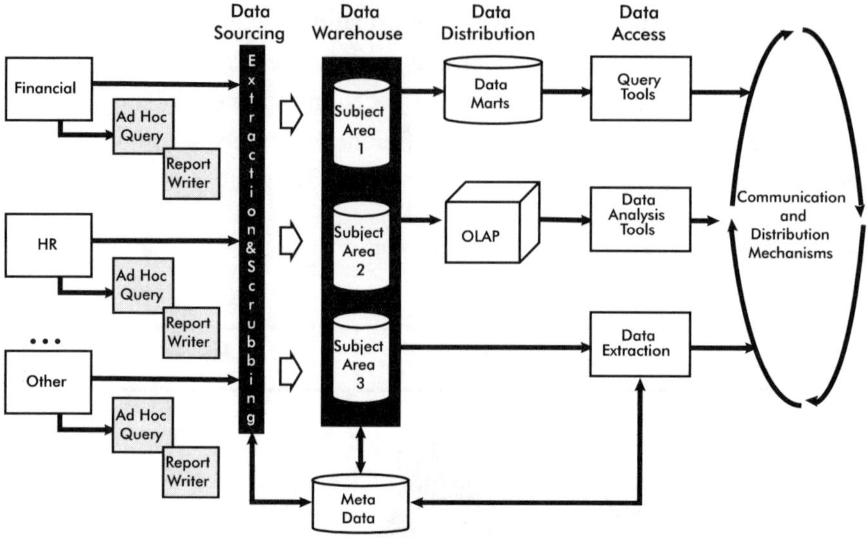

WAR ROOM

The war room is a state-of-the-art element in effective planning as we saw in the EastJet example in Chapter Eight. The tools for understanding and improving value alone will not create value. What is needed is a vehicle to help management use those data tools. The war room is often misunderstood because organizations frequently perceive their conference room to be a war room. We define a war room in the traditional military sense—as a central location where all information about the enterprise and the competitive marketplace resides in real time and current form, for all serious decision makers to observe. It is one of the oldest and best proven management devices and is the embodiment of real-time planning, as you can appreciate in this excerpt about a telecommunications company profiled in *FORTUNE*:

> Each workday morning at 6:00 a.m., Ron Serrano gets a wake-up call from an outfit that reads every newspaper and watches every TV advertisement in Connecticut. The caller tells him if any of his competitors in the telephone industry have come up with a new service or gimmick

that will lure precious customers from the 118-year-old Southern New England Telephone Co., where he is a senior vice president. By 8:00 a.m., the lean, intense Serrano is usually holed up in the "war room" at SNET headquarters overlooking Yale University in New Haven, updating stats on market share, gathering reports and rumors from employees, and plotting strategies. CEO Daniel Miglio, Serrano and a dozen other top officers in the room have given themselves a rule: They have 24 hours to begin delivering a competitive response to any move by a rival. If necessary, they can vent their frustrations by throwing darts at dart boards plastered with symbols of their telephone adversaries—Sprint's Candace Bergen, or MCI's Whoopi Goldberg. Says a weary Serrano: "The gaming, the strategizing. The search for whether the equilibrium of the industry has changed overnight. It never ends. It's certainly never boring." [2]

As SNETs experience shows, an effective war room should have the latest competitive market share information, advertising-spending data and competitive information on cost of goods and pricing, all the relevant data and the value drivers for an organization, captured in such a way that at a moment's notice, decision makers can have up-to-the minute data at their fingertips. In the future, as organizations begin to capture data live, the war room will exist on people's desktops. Until then, it is important that a firm have one central location that contains all the data from which it can make critical decisions. Whether to discuss long-term strategy or short-term tactical moves, the war room enables a company to make rapid decisions aligned with its overall strategy. A recent *FORTUNE* article published a Yankee Group estimate of SNETs long distance market share in its Connecticut market at 30 percent. This is a significant rise from 0 percent three years ago and competing against the likes of AT&T, MCI and Sprint.[3]

The Value Infrastructure and NationJet

NationJet's CEO, George Braga, had become reflective. The meeting in which Vince Gordon dropped his bombshell about customer loyalty statistics shed light on an issue that continued to dog Braga. While Gordon's information and request for funding to capitalize on a value opportunity was exciting, there were elements of it Braga found deeply disturbing. Although in the last year on his Value Journey, he was very proud of many of the accomplishments he had been able to achieve in the organization. Gordon's proposal showed that the inherent lack of infrastructure represented a serious impediment to the organizational progress Braga hoped to accomplish. While he believed the organization had rallied behind him, when he looked beneath the surface, he saw a crumbling infrastructure.

This broken infrastructure was not simple to repair. Each time George Braga had asked his people to identify what would be required to fix the infrastructure, he received proposals for enormous capital projects and very long timeframes to make permanent repairs. As such, the last year had been a series of big proposals followed by band-aid reactions just to keep the infrastructure limping along. He recognized that this was not sustainable and, in fact, the infrastructure had to be the platform from which his organization would one day run. The current infrastructure could not support his long-term vision.

While this was a daunting task, Braga took a logical approach to evaluating the infrastructure at a simple and high level view. He thought about making value the mission. There were infrastructure elements that he believed would be particularly necessary. The first was people and more specifically communications: his belief was that internal and external communications had been inconsistent and not understood well enough to be a rallying point for the company's customers, employees and shareholders. As such, his belief was that he would need to alter his message and continue to reinforce that message at every opportunity. He believed that the overhaul of the communications plan was something that was a very high priority and could be implemented rapidly.

The second critical element in the people category was providing an environment of continuous learning. The challenge here was that both existing training programs and in fact a commitment to learning were scattered and spotty and while he felt his senior management team had embraced the concept of value, he recognized that the remaining manager level and line employees were only vaguely familiar with how a value organization works. Evolving NationJet into a company driving (or more correctly, flying) towards continuous organizational learning would be slow but, certainly, will be a very high priority if he was to succeed.

Braga thought about the value scorecards that he has put in place. While he had focused managers on correct outcomes, there were significant data gaps in the organization. His financial data, as presented, was not very flexible. He continued to be told by his systems people that the financial information he asked for required significant manual efforts on a recurring basis and to support the one-off studies. As information requests in this new value-focused environment increased, the Information Systems (IS) department was collapsing under its own weight. Delays in systems changes had skyrocketed and queuing time for requests had become unworkable. Each time he addressed this issue he was told that the organization needed an enterprise-wide financial system—a key element in the tools and technology category of value infrastructure—that entirely started from a clean sheet of paper. Similarly, the customer data and people data were woefully inadequate. During the past year IS had consolidated data collection but had yet to scratch the surface in any meaningful way. NationJet's inability to support the value scorecard, began to gnaw at Braga. These were enormous tasks to build the data infrastructure and the people were now clambering for data that did not exist.

Significant process changes were at the heart of the problem. As such, the next element for consideration was the activities an organization undertakes to create value for its employees, customers and shareholders. While the existing activity based costing system (ABC) was imperfect, George Braga had gotten workable feedback and could adapt it to support the value perspective. As such, he listed the ABC requirements as a lower value priority and something that could very quickly be adjusted to support the value scorecard.

The next element involved the creation and population of the value models themselves. While he was comfortable with the results of the new business models and the resulting issues, he recognized that his airline still did not have the competency to build and maintain the models. Many of the tools required were not standard fare throughout management. While the scale of these infrastructure elements were far less grave than some of the systems work, they were important elements to getting where he needed to go. Developing modeling competency was recognized to be a high priority item, but one that could be reasonably slow as it was a competency that had not been emphasized in the past. Modeling tools were readily available in the commercial marketplace and, as such, would be a lower priority item that could be obtained in very short order.

Braga also realized that the reporting and analysis function within his organization was not strong. Even with the data and information brought to the forefront, there was no process in place to analyze systematically and report on a routine basis the performance of the organization. This was particularly disturbing because the organization now understood what it wanted to measure and how performance would drive value, but it was simply unable to provide the reporting infrastructure to meet these needs.

Considerable confusion also existed about whether historical performance against value drivers was good enough. Gaining an understanding of what drove value and how to measure it was only part of the journey. The organization then needed to provide benchmarks and best practices to serve as targets so that target setting became an important part of the management process. These benchmarks needed to be value-tested or they would be meaningless as performance measure targets. Braga recognized that reengineering the reporting and analysis function was a high priority and, once again, a long-term project. He recognized, however, that targeting best practices and benchmarks to performance management could be accomplished quickly.

Braga was still concerned about support for his value-based compensation program. The requirements here were simple: those who create value should share in the rewards. The missing element was a systematic and comprehensive way to obtain competitive market salary information for the employee base. This area represented a lower priority but could be quickly remedied.

The final area in Braga's value program was planning. He recognized this as a high-priority element of value creation but one that was not easy to achieve. Planning needed a complete overhaul. Finally, his ultimate vision for planning process, a war room, seemed to be a distant goal because so many of the pieces were missing. Building a war room that reported blanks would not be enlightening.

Figure 9.4 outlines Braga's thoughts on infrastructure. This picture represents more than a simple fire alarm; it is a depressing depiction of how

Figure 9.4   NationJet's Infrastructure Needs

	Slow	Fast
High	Flexible Financial system (Enterprise-wide System Replacement) Customer Value Data People Value Data Continuous Organizational Learning Modeling Competency Reporting and Analysis Reengineering Planning Process Reengineering	Communications
Low	**War Room**	Activity Based Costing Modeling Tools Benchmarks and Best Practices Competitive Market Pricing

Value Priority

Implementation Timing

badly the infrastructure served a company trying to deliver a value approach to managing. Braga was wondering whether, in fact, he could make it. These initiatives represented the foundation on which he would build. Yet all his high-priority items required long-term, expensive projects. He knew the company's survival depended on effectively managing this list of priorities because there wasn't enough money to undertake it all simultaneously.

Three options came to mind. The first was to undertake all the initiatives and decide to bet big that he could remake the infrastructure. This was an expensive proposition but represented the gamble that could allow him to take the organization to a new level. He could not afford the risk of a "big bang" approach. The second option was incremental, balancing short- and long-term, and in fact represented a smaller bet with interim results. The second option would build some infrastructure bridges and short-term solutions while long-term design was under way. This, in some respects, seems the more palatable option but would have to be carefully managed. A third option was to continue with business as usual and hope that over time, as the airline replaced systems and infrastructure, it will do the right thing. This approach could take a long time and destroy plenty of value along the way.

After thinking about his options for a while, George Braga recognized that his best opportunity lay in the incremental approach to infrastructure change, with a series of smaller investments and interim results. After reviewing his wall chart, he decided that while using an incremental approach he needed to think about the changes necessary to provide some of the interim solutions while his long-term road map guided him towards his vision. Figure 9.5 represents Braga's execution plan.

Figure 9.5   Revised NationJet Priorities

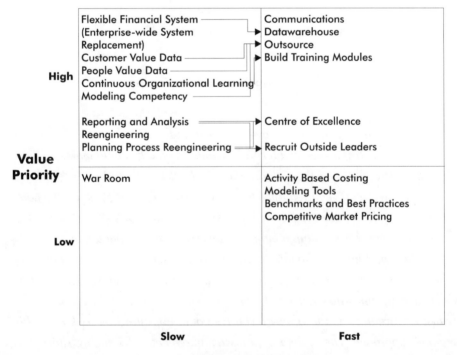

While an enterprise-wide financial system overhaul was under way, NationJet looked at data warehousing as an interim solution to get more flexible and timely information. Braga contracted out customer-value data, the people-value data and modeling competency. While this was not a long-term solution, there were experts in the field who could provide immediate results while the organization learned how to generate and maintain robust data. To foster a continuous organizational learning, Braga felt the competency gaps were identifiable and the key opportunities were evident. He felt comfortable developing some training modules to bridge those gaps. Finally, the two reengineering initiatives he thought were necessary could be supplemented in the near term by taking the most competent resources and developing a center of excellence to support multiple organizational units. He will provide outside recruits who can serve as leaders and catalysts.

For some of the quick hits, his decisions were easier. The activity-based costing system was left as is and changes made only as required. NationJet would buy modeling tools. He would outsource benchmarking and best-practice development to experts with databases that would be readily available while NationJet aligned with noncompeting organizations to share information. The program compared NationJet's reservation center against the best in reservations class of the hotel industry, then against airline competitors. It would compare the other organizations' structures, costs and average numbers of complaints per 1,000 calls, employees hired per 1,000 calls, and the ratio of full- to part-time workers. Finally, NationJet outsourced the competitive market pricing of employees' compensation packages. The findings showed George Braga that by investing in new technology, giving more authority to call-centre employees and hiring more part-timers, the result would be quantifiable improvements in customer satisfaction and lower costs.

This program represented a considerable "to do" list, but Braga felt that the remaining pieces would be manageable and would get him some of the necessary infrastructure to continue to evolve his organization's evolution to a value enterprise.

He decided to give up the concept of the war room in the near term but still held visions that, once the information became available, he could very quickly build his war room. For now he would focus on his actionable "to do" list.

George Braga is now feeling much more confident about the airline's path ahead. While the obstacles are still great, he has a road map in mind that will provide him with a long-term view to rebuilding his organizational infrastructure. He also has a short-term "to do" list identified and ready to execute. All the high-priority value requirements have been supplemented with program fixes that will allow the organization to make significant progress in the near term while waiting for the ultimate solution to come to fruition. While he is certain that there will be new changes and challenges that will create the need for rapid response in the years ahead, he feels confident that his organization understands the goal, is focused on the right outcomes and is actually managing the drivers of value in a business to achieve those outcomes. Managers and line workers have an understanding of where and how they can make a difference in the organization to create value. Their individual and collective performance is being measured and compensation is tied to where and how they create enterprise value.

World-class companies that have a rapid cycle of converting data to information and analysis to decisions depend on value models for their guidelines. They have rich frameworks, a tendency toward creating new data as decisions evolve but also of discarding much of the old and of identifying data gaps for systematic bridging. What they have is a robust and dynamic framework where, as information needs change, systems adapt. The systems become a competitive weapon not only for product launch but for faster and more comprehensive, holistic decision making.

A sluggish process bureaucracy cannot exist in a value enterprise. The infrastructure must reflect the immediacy of the marketplace. For example, in the case of a software company with dropping sales, if it takes 15 to 30 days to get last month's sales numbers, a substantial amount of value destruction will have taken place before anyone is even aware there is a problem. One of our telecommunication clients suffered from process bureaucracy which was a continual problem for the executives in charge of business divisions. One of them said that he couldn't ever explain last month's sales results beyond an intuition, because he had to wait three months for finance to distribute key operational data such as volume growth and market share. His frustration was that the organization was not aligned for speed, but rather for accuracy. Finance's viewpoint was that it's better to wait and get the right number as opposed to getting a number that is 95 percent accurate in three days. The trade-off between speed and precision is one that all organizations must cope with. The value models and the gravity of your decision should guide any trade-off between more speed or more accuracy, or whether the company should focus on precision to the third significant digit.

Once a company aligns its processes with customer value it can free itself from vague intuition. It can base its actions on facts. At that point, the company can begin to confidently allocate financial capital, human capital, and managerial energy toward decisions and activities that support the customer value attributes that have the highest impacts and thus, the best potential for value creation in a timely fashion.

People, process, tools and technology come together to form an effective value framework. With modeling as a screen for relevant data, the infrastructure elements combine to create an agile organizational framework that fosters real-time planning and flexibility. And perhaps most importantly, the value infrastructure will demand that the company thoroughly understand the people side of its business—the customer, whose value proposition is always priority, and the employees, whose capabilities and creativity are recognized as the primary drivers of your organization's value.

Chapter 10

THE SUCCESSFUL VALUE ENTERPRISE

Becoming the Company You Want to Be

Creating a value enterprise is a never-ending journey, and this book provides only a glimpse of the beginning of that journey. Creating value for an organization is not a new idea, although it has become more popular lately. Some would call it a fashion or a fad, but that is unfair because "fad" implies something trivial and unimportant. There are many fads, or flavors of the moment, in business management literature. Most of these limit themselves to one facet of a business enterprise. Value-based management is different. It is a comprehensive discipline, a conceptually sound framework for doing business by balancing customers, shareholders and employees, while finding value opportunities across white space and business unit boundaries. Unlike other value theories, the value enterprise links the conceptual with the actual. It provides a real framework, actual tools and actual techniques to arrive at an integrated, holistic approach to value creation, instead of focusing on just one dimension.

Clients who work on their Value Journey frequently ask, "How will we know when we get there?" To help in illustrating the goal, a set of criteria have been developed as a basis to judge progress. A company becomes a value enterprise when:

- The people in the organization understand value-based management principles and concepts and are applying them through a common language of value.

- The business segments have identified their value drivers and measures and are using them to assess their performance.

- Value concepts are imbedded in key management functions of the business including planning and budgeting, resource allocation, reporting and analysis and performance assessment.

- Value-based decision support tools have been developed and are being applied in making key decisions.

- New investments and programs are value tested before being implemented.

- Compensation is linked to the creation of value at all levels of the organization.

- The company is creating value in the commercial marketplace and realizing that value in the capital marketplace.

These are ambitious goals but they are achievable. Some of the holistic, value-creating examples cited in this book are now examined.

In the past seven years, Wal-Mart's growth has begun to flatten, causing its returns on total capital and net worth to slip. Whereas earnings once grew at 20 to 25 percent annually, recently that figure has been closer to 10 to 15 percent. The main reasons: saturation of its market prospects in the US, increased competition and general overcapacity in the retail market. As well, its forays into other countries—Argentina, Brazil, Mexico, China, Indonesia and Canada—have been less profitable because of the small scale of the endeavors and, in the case of Mexico, because of the collapse of the peso. In the United States, Wal-Mart has responded by expanding its line of superstores that will add perishable food to the store inventories. Because this is a new line for Wal-Mart and outside its core competency, there is greater risk. But Wal-Mart's stock still trades at a 21 percent premium to the market, despite a weak dividend payout. And the company has shown improvement in cash flow. Wal-Mart's value culture means that it is in a strong position to deal with the problems it faces, far more than other retailers that do not have value-based management.

General Electric, widely accepted as one of the greatest value-creating companies of all time, cited Wal-Mart in its 1992 annual report as an example of superb value creation:

> In 1991, we shared best practices with a number of great companies.
> We learned something everywhere, but nowhere did we learn as much

as at Wal-Mart. Sam Walton and his strong team are something very special. Many of our management teams spent time observing the speed, the bias for action, the utter customer fixation that drives Wal-Mart; and despite our progress, we came back feeling a bit plodding and ponderous, a little envious, but ultimately, fiercely determined that we're going to do whatever it takes to get that fast.[1]

The value-based organization is one in which there is a balanced approach to managing a business and a framework reflecting that balance. As Wal-Mart's current experience shows, organizations will always have big challenges or developments under way that will threaten balance. For many companies, it is impossible simply to wipe their slate clean and fill it with all new value programs. How can an organization reconcile the unevenness in the pursuit of becoming a value enterprise? Becoming a value enterprise is truly a journey that may never have a defined end. A value enterprise is constantly a work in progress in which successes will reveal themselves incrementally and in fits and starts. Acknowledging this from the beginning will help make sense of the unevenness of the pursuit that every company will inevitably face.

Throughout the journey a company should keep in mind the key concepts discussed in this book that produce a holistic value-management framework. This book described the need for balance among a company's constituencies. Achieving this balance is not simple, and in fact, a company may always have the sense that there is a continual imbalance despite its efforts. Balancing constituencies comes about by making sure that a company recognize equally the value of its customers, shareholders and employees—not value relative to one another, or in the sense of giving each one equal time and effort, but, value within each constituency's marketplace. This means making sure that each receives a value proposition that meets or exceeds what is offered by the competition. When this is accomplished for customers, employees and shareholders, an organization is on track for value creation.

The necessity of making value a corporate mission, from the boiler room to the boardroom, is critical. That means making value the company's culture. Value must be a company's stated goal, but it must also be woven into a company's day-to-day existence if it is to have a real impact. If value is the company's mission, the culture must be attuned to value creation at virtually every level.

The merits of the value scorecard make it the best indicator of an organization's ability to create value, both in the present and in the future. Great companies have known that cash flow is the purest measure of value performance and the notion of economic profit has been around for decades. But what distinguishes a value enterprise in this realm is its rigorous approach to installing a value scorecard combining measures for shareholders, customers and employees at every level of your organization. This comprehensive approach ultimately results in world-class performance measurement.

As discussed, modeling is the cornerstone of a true value enterprise. It requires a huge commitment to become a learning organization in a comprehensive way. Once a company commits to and undertakes modeling, it becomes one of an elite group of enterprises that has an unsurpassed level of knowledge in virtually all areas of operation. Its performance measurement processes recognize that organizations do not deal exclusively in qualitative analysis, but that certain things need to be tracked mathematically, and that a quantitative construct is important to implementation.

Value-based compensation is probably the most misunderstood part of value management. Some organizations have gone from having no mechanism for pay at risk or linkage with shareholders, to a situation where there is risk in the compensation plan, but without employee control over performance. A value-compensation plan puts some risk in the game, but the overall focus is to devise a compensation plan for every employee level based on that person's ability to influence value. When people at every level know how their day-to-day efforts affect value drivers for their company, compensation becomes relevant to all, and tangible efforts are rewarded in an equitable way.

Value-based planning, meanwhile, recognizes that all organizations eventually evolve into having a planning function, some more formal than others. Because of this, a company must maintain a value-based perspective in planning. But the key is an untraditional approach not governed by the calendar. Everyone must be taught the fundamentals of recognizing value, and then understand that value is created through ongoing, competitive responses. When this perspective is accomplished, the idea of anytime, anywhere planning—real-time planning—becomes possible.

A value enterprise must be prepared to invest in its infrastructure to help people execute value decisions more effectively. In mature organizations, the existing infrastructure can be very expensive to replace. But young companies possessing state-of-the-art data capture often outperform long-time industry leaders. Replacing an outdated infrastructure is clearly critical to survival.

One of the finest examples of a value enterprise, is the journey undertaken by Jack Welch, CEO of General Electric. His words indicate the balanced approach he's taken to create a value enterprise.

> The three most important things you need to measure in a business are customer satisfaction, employee satisfaction and cash flow. If you are growing customer satisfaction, your global market share is sure to grow too. Employee satisfaction gets you productivity, quality, pride and creativity. Cash flow is the pulse—the vital sign of life in a company.

Jack Welch is the gold standard against which all CEOs are measured. Currently his company is the most valuable one in the world, with a total market capitalization of $157 billion. An examination of the Value Journey that GE undertook during Welch's tenure indicates that his strategy was not only a clear plan for value creation, but demonstrated deep understanding of a value program's elements and the dynamic nature of value drivers throughout the enterprise.

When GE's Value Journey began in 1982, Welch declared that his company would be the first or second in each of its key businesses—technology, services and manufacturing—or it would vacate that business. He wanted a particular feel for his company, with the leanness, simplicity and agility enjoyed by small companies. These ideas were badly needed at GE, where negative characteristics were reflected in financial analysts' criticisms that it was a typical conglomerate, picking up and discarding businesses on apparent whims. The result was inconsistent performance on the stock market where GE's price failed to keep pace with its actual achievements.

Welch set about cutting through layers of management, reducing them to as few as four in some businesses, and encouraging those who remained to act faster on everything from inventory turnover, to the time spent on product R&D, to faster responses to customers' needs. By the dawn of the 1990s, GE was experimenting with what Welch called the "boundaryless" company—a firm where suppliers have intimate contact with it as trusted partners, a firm where customers are no longer considered just end users but GE's lifeblood, a firm where customer service becomes the task of every single manager and employee. In Welch's boundaryless environment, the silos began to fade, and functions melded into a seamless operation, which he characterized as "one room, one coffeepot, one team, one shared mission." He put together teams with people drawn from different functions to make new products and services. "Perhaps the biggest stride we've made," he told shareholders, "has been [...] in wringing out 'not-invented-here' from our culture. Increasingly, GE people are now searching, around the world, for better ways of doing things."

GE thus began breaking down its barriers and destroying the encrustation of bureaucracy and often ludicrous activities and protocols large corporations build up: wasteful paperwork, layers of approvals and duplication of work. It enlisted the advice of suppliers and even its customers on how it could improve its activities. One outgrowth was the "Quick Market Intelligence" initiative, which empowered each salesperson with direct weekly access to key managers and the CEO so they could present customer problems and needs. The point was to respond to customers' needs immediately and effectively, but it has had the ancillary effect of focusing everyone's attention on what happens in the marketplace.

Welch made sure that GE rewarded its employees with stock options. These options gave employees a direct link between their performance and the company's success, what he described as "rewards felt in the soul as well as the wallet."

Since then, GE has untapped a vast repository of creativity among employees at all levels. It has become a nimble, highly focused company attentive to the needs of its employees, shareholders and customers. And in 1995, Welch set a new goal for his company: to become a rapid-growth company, a remarkable evolution for a century-old organization like GE. As he told shareholders, "We wanted to build [...] a hybrid, an enterprise with the reach and resources of a big company—the body of a big company—but the thirst to learn, the compulsion to share and the bias for action—the soul—of a small company."

GE has learned the lessons of becoming a value enterprise well. It continues to evolve, to hone its strengths, to raise the bar of its own expectations as well as those of its stakeholders. This will never end, for the Value Journey has no conclusion. The odyssey for other companies will also be long, but it can be just as rewarding as GE's. Value-based management is a framework for managing, but not a prescription. It helps an organization see where and how all the pieces fit together, but it will not explain specifically how to fix something that is broken. The value enterprise recognizes that people must be provided with the freedom to take a proactive view of the marketplace. This can be accomplished by ensuring that everyone at every level truly understands where and how value is created. Once this understanding has been captured organizationally, value enterprise will become a reality. Some companies become so preoccupied with attaining the perfect value plan and the perfect concepts in the perfect timetable, that the crucial ability to proactively jump in with a willingness to learn and make mistakes is frozen. They should focus on reaction time as well as a willingness to separate the roles of architect, designer and builder, that is, a willingness to play each of those roles depending on circumstances within the industry.

A value program is a major undertaking that requires considerable commitment and constant refreshing. Organizations that have a unifying framework and a willingness to react and move forward quickly with that framework are the ones that will create sustained value over the long term. Recognition of the need to apply a consistent framework is the first step in the journey to becoming a value enterprise.

APPENDIX
Value Enterprise Compared to Other Programs

As a company begins its value-based management journey, it will probably wonder how it can integrate existing management trends that it may have implemented, such as a Total Quality Management (TQM) or reengineering. Value-based management enables a company to examine the activities generated by current management trends and how effective they really are. Eric Abrahamson, author of "Management Fashion" in the January 1996 issue of *Academy of Management Review*, states that management trends, implemented at the right time and in the proper amounts can be good, because they force managers to think of new ways to work.[1] In addition, value-based management, with its holistic framework, can bind together management trends or subject them to rigorous examination so that a company can decide whether it is the best course for the organization. It is important to embrace trends and fashions that truly reflect a company's needs, but from a value perspective.

Consider some of the following management trends viewed from a value perspective.

TOTAL QUALITY MANAGEMENT/CUSTOMER FOCUS

TQM seeks to design an organization that meets or exceeds customer expectations. If a company figures out what its customer requirements are and works back from that perspective through every area of the company, there will be plenty of value created for shareholders and employees, as well as customers. TQM's focus on customer value is directly aligned with the value-based approach discussed in Chapter Five, but focusing merely on customers to create value can be misguided. In many organizations, TQM programs eat up money on equipment and processes. Value-based management advocates balancing a company's constituencies equally. Exceeding customer expectations could be taken to the extreme by deeply cutting prices, but the balance for shareholders and employees would then clearly be destroyed. There must be a balance in trade-offs. Going too far in any one direction only creates other problems. Finding the balance is critical and very much a value based approach.

REENGINEERING

Reengineering prescribes changing and redesigning the way a business operates to achieve results. It could affect the entire company and its activities or just a part, depending on the nature of the change. Reengineering is popular because it helps companies transform from compartmentalized, vertical organizations full of functional silos, to horizontal, process-focused ones. In this way, reengineering is an ally of the value-based approach. But its shortcoming is that it does not spell out exactly what needs to be reengineered and for what reason. Without a holistic business-driven objective like value creation, *what* needs to be reengineered may not be fully evident or consistent. Using a value-based model to see the gaps in initiatives, and understanding the relationships between processes and value can focus reengineering projects and provide a rational basis for prioritization. Change is a good thing, as long as it creates value rationally and logically. In this way, reengineering is a complimentary process to value-based management.

OUTSOURCING, VIRTUAL CORPORATIONS AND CORE COMPETENCY FOCUS

Every successful business has defining characteristics that are central to its success. There are other functions not critical to its success but which must be performed, such as payroll and payment processing. These functions could ostensibly be contracted out without having an impact on the company's success. This refers to trends known variously as outsourcing non core competencies or creating a virtual corporation. They focus on the factors that are crucial to an organization's success. Rather than fixing something, as reengineering does, this discipline dispenses with the unnecessary. Pillsbury's Green Giant division examined its core competencies and decided that marketing packaged food and managing retail channels were its strong suits. They could outsource their packaging and even their growing fields without damage to the product or their image. So the Valley of the Green Giant is now managed by someone else; the frozen corn and peas are packaged by someone else, and only the marketing and distribution are handled by Pillsbury. This is an example of how a virtual corporation works. From a value perspective, this discipline is a compelling possibility for value creation. But if outsourcing damages the employee constituency, a company should look for an acceptable balance.

EMPOWERMENT AND QUALITY CIRCLES

Empowerment recognizes that employees are a firm's greatest resource and when given freedom and responsibility, their capabilities are unlimited. Quality circles foster discussions by small groups of volunteer employees on specific work-related assessments. The idea behind quality circles and empowerment is that workers will always be more productive and more prone to give their best effort when they are operating in an empowering environment. This is a method of fostering an employee value approach and is in line with value-based management principles. Indeed, empowerment is one of the more compelling of current management trends. When employees are not only empowered to act and understand how value is created, but also empowered as owners who are aligned with shareholders, the benefits can be tremendous.

JUST-IN-TIME INVENTORY (JIT) CONTROL

This discipline changes inventory procedures so that very little of any product is carried until just before it is needed. JIT companies negotiate long-term contracts with a few chosen suppliers located as close to the production facility as possible so that inventories can be purchased and delivered just in time to be distributed. JIT reduces working capital tied up in inventory and seeks greater product movement efficiency. Its proponents say that it is far more than an inventory control procedure, that failure to control inventory is symptomatic of larger problems; the need for JIT is just one aspect of this. However, if JIT is practised so strictly as to impede a company's flexibility when unexpected opportunities arise, it can be detrimental. For example, if a company has a significant shortfall of supply in a period of increasing demand, it would clearly be to its advantage to have inventory sitting around. Under those circumstances, the company may want to capitalize on the opportunity in the marketplace by ignoring its JIT principles. Capturing fast-breaking value opportunity is sometimes difficult under JIT-type programs.

ACTIVITY-BASED COSTING

An activity-based cost system helps a company better understand the things that drive cost in its organization. It can focus on those activities that might offer opportunities for savings through efficiency, simplification or elimination. A management trend called activity-based management is emerging. It builds on activity-based costing by taking an expanded look at the benefits of activities as well as their cost. Value-based management also looks at the benefit as well as the cost. If activity-based management looked at capital assets and working capital as value-based management does, and also recognized the importance of the cash flow perspective, the two disciplines would be very much the same. Unfortunately, it often doesn't.

BALANCED SCORECARD

This approach to performance measurement stresses that a company should not look strictly at financial measures of success or any other measure that is narrow in scope. It asserts that performance should reflect all important areas, and only in this way will the performance scorecard be balanced. In their work on the balanced scorecard, two Harvard University professors, Robert Kaplan and David Norton, made the concept popular. It is sound in theory, but in practice is implemented differently. Often companies simply advise visiting each functional part of a company to discover factors that are essential to success for each area, then build a scorecard that centers on those findings. This seems satisfactory until you address the problem of functional hierarchies. When soliciting information from each department, it may be that only that department's narrow view of the world is incorporated, without the insight of trade-offs and interrelationships between various parts of the enterprise. As mentioned earlier, very often an improvement in one area of an organization comes at the expense of another. Understanding trade-offs is critical to a comprehensive view, but the best way they will be revealed accurately, is through the exercise of modeling. If modeling is done correctly, a balanced scorecard of performance measures will be the natural outcome of the exercise rather than something that must be sought.

BENCHMARKING

This is about making comparisons. It enables a company to see how it compares to its competitors and others in the industry, and then provides a basis for improvement, which, of course, is always a positive thing. The one cautionary note is that a company must be sure it is comparing apples to apples. For example, if a company has a core business and also a subsidiary, benchmarking must be used carefully to ensure that the comparisons include only the core business or only the subsidiary, depending on the information being sought. Done properly, this is a useful tool to assist in determining value-creation opportunities as well as providing targets for performance assessment.

THE LEARNING ORGANIZATION

This concept suggests that we live in a world full of opportunities to learn. Made popular by Peter Senge's book, *The Fifth Discipline*,[2] it advocates a series of disciplines to better understand the organization and improve its ability to adapt. This clearly is consistent with modeling and the Value Journey to becoming more aware of the nature of the organization. Given this, perhaps the number one competency a business should develop is organizational speed. How fast can it learn and how fast can it change? A company's ability to learn quickly is a valuable skill that could give it a clear competitive advantage. Unlike other management concepts, this one has not been put in place as effectively as reengineering or TQM. This is unfortunate since it may be the most important management trend of all. The learning organization is challenging because it is holistic and thus is a good fit with the value perspective. If a company is dealing with the mass market, it might focus its learning on how to understand customers' taste and preference changes quickly. Each company will focus on that which is unique to its business. A value framework coupled with learning-organization concepts will speed the process.

CHANGE MANAGEMENT

Not so much a concept as a recognition, change management states that organizations have difficulty changing. In some respects, resistance to change is good because organizations need to be consistent to be efficient. But there also must be capacity to adapt as the world changes. Thus, a real need exists to manage change effectively, whether it is through TQM, reengineering or other ways. It is common in business today for most major initiatives to have some change-management program that goes with it. In the context of value-based management, change management is a key "enabler." Once a company identifies the changes it needs from a value-based perspective, it can use change management as a basis for getting there. Value-based management can serve as the powerful change imperative for organizations. Once people start to recognize that they will not be in business if they do not make the value grade for customers, shareholders and employees, they will have a strong imperative for change.

Management trends such as these tend to address fragments of the life of a corporation. But value-based management can bind them together or cast a common objective over their actual utility in a company. In fact, while several of these management approaches are necessary and useful at points in time, value-based management can and should be used to integrate the programs to ensure a common goal, and to create value for the organization and its stakeholders.

Management trends come and go, but good basic business fundamentals always remain in style. The holistic nature of value-based management is clearly not a trend that is here today and gone tomorrow. It is something that intuitive managers in successful companies have been doing for a long time.

ENDNOTES

CHAPTER 1

1. Alex Taylor III, "Boeing: Sleepy in Seattle", *FORTUNE*, August 7, 1995.

2. Philip Condit, "Focusing on the Customer: How Boeing Does It," *Management*, January-February 1994.

3. J.P. Donlon, "Boeing's Big Bet", *Chief Executive*, Nov-Dec, 1994, 40-44

4. Alex Taylor III, "Boeing: Sleepy in Seattle", *FORTUNE*, August 7, 1995.

5. Andrew Osterland, "Big Enough", *Financial World*, April 15, 1997

6. Michael Skapkinker, "Boeing the Boss Despite Brave Forces", *Financial Times of London*, December 16, 1996, 26.

7. Andrew Osterland, "Big Enough", *Financial World*, April 15, 1997

8. All Cognos information has been drawn from Cognos' Annual Reports, 1994-97

9. "Leading the Cognos Clan into Battle", *The Ottawa Citizen*, October 10, 1996

CHAPTER 2

1. Robert D. Buzzell and Bradley T. Gale, *The PIMS Principles: Linking Strategy to Performance*, (New York: Free Press, 1987), 7.

2. Jeffrey Pffefer, *Competitive Advantage Through People: Unleashing the Power of the Work Force,* (Boston: Harvard Business School Press, 1994).

3. Ibid.

4. Marjorie Kelly, "Business Ethics," *Minneapolis Star-Tribune,* March 25, 1996.

5. All Wal-Mart interview quotations are drawn from Jay L Johnson, "How Wal-Mart's People Make a Difference", *Discount Merchandiser,* August, 1993, 60-63.

6. Thomas A. Stewart, *Intellectual Capital: The New Wealth of Organizations,* (New York: Currency Doubleday, 1997).

7. Gary McWilliams, "Whirlwind on the Web," *BusinessWeek*, April 7, 1997, 136.

CHAPTER 3

1. Robert Carey, "Wired and Weird", *Successful Meetings,* September, 1994, 62-71.

2. Jonathan Burton, "Lesson No. 1: Learning from the Customer", *Chief Executive*, March, 1996, 58-59.

3. Matthew Kreitman, "Doing the Continental", *Airfinance Journal,* June 1996, 14-16.

4. Wendy Zellner, "The Right Place, The Right Time," *BusinessWeek*, May 27, 1996, page 74.

5. Ibid.

CHAPTER 4

1. Shlomo Maital, *Executive Economics: Ten Essential Tools for Managers,* (New York: Free Press, 1994), 70, 52.

2. Alfred Rappaport, *Creating Shareholder Value: The New Standard for Business Performance*, (New York: Free Press, 1986), 44.

3. Harvey Davis, *Cash Flow and Performance Measurement: Managing for Value*, (Morristown: Financial Executives Research Foundation, 1996), 78.

4. Chris Gussel, "Why Book Value Doesn't Mean So Much", *Investor's Daily*, November 21, 1996, A1.

5. Harvey Davis, *Cash Flow and Performance Measurement: Managing for Value*, (Morristown: Financial Executives Research Foundation, 1996), 165.

CHAPTER 5

1. Jay W. Forrester, *Industrial Dynamics*, (Portland, Oregon: Productivity Press, 1961), 43. Originally published by MIT Press, Cambridge, Mass.

2. Peter M. Senge, *The Fifth Discipline: The Art and Practice of the Learning Organization*, (New York: Currency Doubleday, 1990), 69.

3. Jay W. Forrester, *Industrial Dynamics*, (Portland, Oregon: Productivity Press, 1961), 56. Originally published by MIT Press, Cambridge, Mass.

4. Peter M. Senge, *The Fifth Discipline: The Art and Practice of the Learning Organization*, (New York: Currency Doubleday, 1990), 24.

5. Ibid., 281

6. Ibid., 174

7. John Sterman, in Peter Senge et al., *The Fifth Discipline Fieldbook: Strategies and Tools for Building a Learning Organization*, (New York: Currency Doubleday, 1994), 177.

8. John H. Holland, *Hidden Order: How Adaptation Builds Complexity*, (Reading, Mass.: Addison-Wesley, 1995), 11.

9. Peter Schwartz, *The Art of the Long View*, (New York: Currency Doubleday, 1991), 9.

CHAPTER 7

1. "Levi's Offers Year's Pay as Incentive Bonus", *Los Angeles Times,* June 13, 1996.

2. Ibid.

CHAPTER 8

1. James Brian Quinn, *Intelligent Enterprise: A Knowledge and Service Based Paradigm for Industry*, (New York: Free Press, 1992).

2. W. Kiechel, III, Sniping at Strategic Planning, *Planning Review*, May 1984: 8–11.

3. Henry Mintzberg, *The Rise and Fall of Strategic Planning: Reconceiving Roles for Planning, Plans, Planners*, (New York: Free Press, 1994), 255.

4. James Brian Quinn, *Intelligent Enterprise: A Knowledge and Service Based Paradigm for Industry*, (New York: Free Press, 1992), 109.

5. John A. Byrne, Strategic Planning, *Business Week*, August 26, 1996, 46-52.

6. Ibid., 46.

7. Ibid., 50.

8. Ibid., 50.

9. Ibid., 52.

CHAPTER 9

1. Peter Senge, *The Fifth Discipline: The Art and Practice of the Learning Organization*, (New York: Currency Doubleday, 1990).

2. Brian O'Reilly, "First Blood in the Telecom Wars," *FORTUNE*, March 4, 1996, 124.

3. Ibid

CHAPTER 10

1. All General Electric quotations are drawn from GE Annual Reports, 1992-96.

APPENDIX

1. Eric Abrahamson, "Management Fashion," *Academy of Management Review*, January 1996.

2. Peter M. Senge, *The Fifth Discipline: The Art and Practice of the Learning Organization*, (New York: Currency Doubleday, 1990).

INDEX